Hidden Courage

Hidden Courage

*Reconnecting Faith and Character
with Mental Wellness*

WILLIAM J. ELENCHIN

WIPF & STOCK · Eugene, Oregon

HIDDEN COURAGE
Reconnecting Faith and Character with Mental Wellness

Copyright © 2009 William J. Elenchin. All rights reserved. Except for brief quotations in critical publications or reviews, no part of this book may be reproduced in any manner without prior written permission from the publisher. Write: Permissions, Wipf and Stock Publishers, 199 W. 8th Ave., Suite 3, Eugene, OR 97401.

Wipf and Stock Publishers
A Division of Wipf and Stock Publishers
199 W. 8th Ave., Suite 3
Eugene, OR 97401

www.wipfandstock.com

ISBN 13: 978-1-60608-111-2

Manufactured in the U.S.A.

*"You will never do anything in this world without courage.
It is the greatest quality of the mind next to honor."*[1]

—ARISTOTLE

"Faithless is he that says farewell when the road darkens."[2]

—GIMLI
IN FELLOWSHIP OF THE RING

*"Be not afraid of life. Believe that life is worth living,
and your belief will help create the fact."*[3]

—WILLIAM JAMES

1. As cited in Thinkexist.com Quotations, copyright ThinkExist 1999–2006, "Aristotle," http://thinkexist.com/quotation/you_will_never_do_anything_in_this_world_without/221791.htm.l.

2. J. R. R. Tolkien, *Fellowship of the Ring,* volume 1 of The Lord of the Rings, (London: Allen and Unwin, 1954), 294. Available online at The Thain's Book, 2003–2008, http://www.tuckborough.net/gimli.html.

3. William James, *The Will to Believe and Other Essays in Popular Philosophy*, "Is Life Worth Living?" (Girard, KS: Haldeman-Julius Publications, 1948), 62. Available online at Questia Media America, Inc., http://www.questia.com/PM.qst?a=o&d=101949511. This citation from Laurence G. Boldt, *Zen Soup: Tasty Morsels of Wisdom from Great Minds East & West* (New York: Penguin Arkana, 1997), 19.

Contents

Acknowledgments xi

Introduction ix

1 From a Moral to Mental Compass 1

2 Faith in Reason 11

3 In Freud We Trust? 18

4 Is Life All about Me? 29

5 Wheat and Weeds 42

6 Closing the Loop 49

7 Reason for Faith 70

8 Character 96

Acknowledgments

I AM deeply grateful to my family for their unwavering support. My wife Kate offered her constant encouragement that this was a valuable project. My son Zach and daughters Mary Kate and Hannah provided daily examples of faith and joy that is purest in those with childlike spirits. My parents Gert and John modeled the virtues that bring peace, strength, and joy.

I must also express my sincere appreciation to my editor, Irene Stoops. Her enthusiasm, persistence, and kindness mirrored much of the content of this book, helping make this sometimes challenging work enjoyable.

Introduction

*"Nurture your minds with great thoughts.
To believe in the heroic makes heroes."*[1]

—Benjamin Disraeli,
Earl of Beaconfield, 1804–1881

"No. Not *a good idea. They have either found Jesus or become cops!"* More than ten years have passed since I first heard these words from a mental health therapist, and I can still feel my mind go numb, as it did when I first tried to make sense of that response. The year was 1996, and I was working as a mental health counselor at a youth residential treatment facility. Most of the young men (ages 14 to 18) were court adjudicated delinquents who had come from severely dysfunctional homes or rough street life.

These kids were good at heart, struggling to find a way of life. They were likable, especially when they let their guard down. It also didn't require much insight to see through their defensive shields, as unpleasant as those barricades were. Resentment, pessimism, deceit, and intemperance marked their conduct and guided their lives. They had behavior problems and life issues that needed to be resolved, which was my primary job as a therapist.

---

1. Benjamin Disraeli, *Coningsby*, Book III, Chapter 1, (New York: W. H. Colyer, 1844), as cited online at BrainyQuote, Xplore, Inc., BrainyMedia, 2001–2004, http://www.brainyquote.com/quotes/quotes/b/q121570.html.

Therapy typically included several weekly individual sessions to discuss and process negative past events. These past events could be generalized into two categories: perpetrator or victim of abuse. In therapy we would talk about these experiences and help the youth understand how they influenced his caustic thoughts and behaviors. Once the youngster realized the logical connection between his past issues and deviant or delinquent actions, we could discuss more healthy and lawful modes of conduct. The simple goal was to replace destructive behavior patterns with socially acceptable ones.

The problem with this approach, as most of those who have worked with troubled youth would agree, is that teenage boys with troubled backgrounds typically reject such calculated attempts to change their behaviors. The harmful and oftentimes heartbreaking abuse these youth experienced as children seared their mind, heart, and soul. Positive behavior changes in these youngsters were the exception rather than the rule. Logic and technique were not enough.

Seeking alternative methods to help these young men find healing, I thought it would be a good idea if we had some successful program graduates visit our teens. Perhaps these prior residents, now grown men, could share insights about moving toward wellness and becoming self-sufficient. I sat down with our program director and asked whether he thought it would be a good idea for us to invite graduates to speak with our kids. He thought for a moment and replied with all sincerity, "No. Not a good idea. They have either found Jesus or become cops!"

Placing faith in a Higher Power or becoming a police officer is *undesirable*? I begin with this story because it is so typical of the view taken by many in the mental health field regarding faith beliefs, character, and mental health. Since this incident occurred I can cite many similar examples from my experience working in the field of behavioral health. The reason for this antagonistic view toward faith is that much current mental health treatment operates from a myopic perspective that addresses the mind with little attention given to the spirit and body.

The majority of individuals who work in the mental health system and receive treatment in that system function within a framework that has historically, perhaps unknowingly, divorced faith beliefs and virtues from psychological health. This separation of religious and spiritual beliefs from good mental health *may* have been necessary to help establish psychology as a serious, scientific discipline. That matter is open to debate. However, a profound outcome of the separation of faith beliefs from the cultural and clinical understanding of mental health has been that religious beliefs have not only been dismissed, but are often seen as a sign of pathology or mental illness! Fortunately, there has been growing research and public interest regarding the relationship between faith beliefs and not only psychological health but physical health as well. During the past decade studies have greatly increased in number and consistently support a positive association between religion or spirituality and overall health. This interest and recognition of the power of faith is slowly filtering down into the treatment of a variety of mental illnesses and is also influencing our cultural view of mental wellness.

It was my frustration with mental health's arrogance toward faith that led me to study this subject in a doctoral program. When I began my studies I questioned whether there would be enough research in academic literature to support the theory that religious beliefs and practices enhance wellness. This uncertainty came from working within a field that virtually shuns religion and character traits as components of mental wellness. To my pleasant surprise I discovered that most academic literature on psychotherapy now acknowledges both the animosity toward religion that has been present since the establishment of psychology as a discipline and that key founding psychological theorists played a pivotal role in demonizing religious beliefs and faith practices. Contemporary research findings have begun to dispel the long-held false assumption that religion and values are incompatible with good mental health and have instead established a connection between faith and wellness.

In addition to those generally interested in behavioral health, this book is intended to reach two primary audiences. The first is individuals who receive mental health services to find relief from psychological difficulties. These emotional challenges include anxiety, depression, grief, alcohol abuse, and addictions. This is in no way a how-to manual for identifying or treating mental illness. Instead, the primary purpose for this book is to dispel the notion that time-honored character traits, which are often taught as part of religious teachings, have no place in mental wellness. Many who cope with emotional struggles believe that the principles of good mental health are the exclusive domain of licensed professionals, and that common virtues such as wisdom, temperance, justice, and courage are separate from mental health. This is simply not the case.

The second audience is behavioral health practitioners—licensed professionals and paraprofessionals—who work to enhance their client's mental well-being. Until recently the majority of mental health educational and training programs have deemed faith and character to be irrelevant if not harmful to psychological wellness. This is out of step with the beliefs of the general public. A 2006 poll conducted by Pew Research Center for the People and the Press and Pew Forum on Public Life found that 96 percent of the population believes in God or some Supreme Being.[2] This high rate of faith has remained constant,

---

2. David Masci and Gregory A. Smith, "God is Alive and Well in America," Pew Forum on Religion and Public Life (Washington D.C.: PewResearchCenter Publications), April 4, 2006, http://pewresearch.org/pubs/15/god-is-alive-and-well-in-america.

even in an increasingly materialistic society, and 42 years after an infamous *Time* magazine article asked "Is God Dead?"[3] It is my hope that mental health professionals will reconsider their treatment models in light of contemporary research supporting religious beliefs and character traits as beneficial to wellness.

In the following pages I occasionally offer an example from my previous work as a counselor to shed light on the nuances that exist in the mental health field. The identifying characteristics have been changed and the events represent an amalgamation of typical experiences to assure anonymity. When I refer to faith beliefs I mostly draw upon Christianity because it has been the predominant religion since our nation's founding and because most emerging research has been conducted with participants influenced by this perspective.

---

3. Ibid.

I

From a Moral to Mental Compass

"We always know that society is full of folly and will deceive us in the matter of humanity. It is an unreliable horse, and blind into the bargain. Woe to the driver if he falls asleep."[1]

—ALBERT SCHWEITZER

DURING THE last year of my Ph.D. program an acquaintance asked me a few questions about a mental health issue relating to his family member. He was aware of my job as a mental health therapist, including prior work as a counselor in two residential treatment facilities. We also had discussed my dissertation research study, which examined depression and spirituality among undergraduate college students. Halfway through the discussion a thought came to his mind and his facial expression changed abruptly. He caught himself and said, "Wait a minute. Your Ph.D. won't be in clinical psychology, will it?" When I affirmed he was correct, he said, "Oh, why am I talking to you about this then!" and immediately ended the discussion.

This incident typifies the societal attitude toward the mental health field. Many believe that the experts possess knowledge unattainable to those outside the field. Solely by earning their

---

1. Albert Schweitzer, *The Philosophy of Civilization*, trans. by C. T. Campion (Buffalo, NY: Prometheus, 1987), 307–29. Chapter 26 online at Chapman University, Schweitzer Institute, http://www.chapman.edu/schweitzerInstitute/revRead/civilization.asp.

degrees, psychologists and psychiatrists have obtained powers of insight that they can use to solve a host of behavior problems. What has fueled this perception, and how has it affected the treatment options?

A COMPARISON WITH MEDICAL SCIENCE

Since the early part of the twentieth century the field of psychology has grown dramatically. Escaping the shadow of philosophy, psychology has developed a cultural standing of prominence and professionalism. From the time of Wilhelm Wundt (1832–1920), who is considered the founder of modern psychology,[2] until the present, psychologists have been keenly interested in applying the scientific method to the understanding of human behaviors. The scientific method is the use of testable experiments and observations to prove a hypothesis, or educated guess, about some phenomenon. This form of inquiry had proven to be highly effective in the natural sciences, such as biology, chemistry, physics, and astronomy. However, it was a new way to gain knowledge for philosophical theorists, who had based much of their previous thinking on opinion and conjecture.

> *"All that is true, by whomever it has been said, has its origin in the Spirit."*[3]
>
> —THOMAS AQUINAS

As a result of this elevated status to professionalism, mental health patients typically assume that the foundations of psychology are as well established as the fundamentals of medical science and that psychological training mirrors medical training.

---

2. Thomas H. Leahey, *A History of Psychology. Main Currents in Psychological Thought*, 2nd ed. (Englewood Cliffs, NJ: Prentice Hall), 1987.

3. As cited in Laurence G. Boldt, *Zen Soup: Tasty Morsels of Wisdom from Great Minds East and West* (New York: Penguin Arkana), 39.

Psychiatrists and psychologists are comparable to medical doctors, therapists are similar to nurses and physicians' assistants, and mental health paraprofessionals match up with medical technicians. Individuals who seek mental health treatment typically assume that they will receive standardized, state-of-the-art care, which flows naturally from an established discipline.

Both professionals and mental health patients have compared psychology to medical science—a field that has made countless valuable advances and saved the lives of an incalculable number by using the regimental scientific method to gain knowledge. One example of a medical advancement is found in the highly contagious smallpox disease that claimed upwards of 500 million lives in the twentieth century. Those who contracted the disease and survived were brutally scarred. An English country doctor named Edward Jenner believed there was some truth in an old wives' tale that milkmaids never contracted smallpox, although they would often come down with the milder disease of cowpox marked by blistered hands. He speculated that it was the pus in the blister that protected the milkmaids from contracting smallpox. In 1796 Jenner set out to prove his theory by injecting pus from a maid's blistered hands into a young boy named James Phipps and repeating the procedure over several days. The doctor's next step was to inject the boy with smallpox. Young Phipps became ill, but within a few days he made a full recovery.

Jenner reported his findings to the medical community in London, and by 1840 the English government endorsed his vaccination as the sole treatment for smallpox. Use of the vaccine spread across the continents, culminating with the World Health Organization's 1980 pronouncement that smallpox was extinct.[4]

4. World Health Organization, "Smallpox eradication: destruction of variola virus stocks. Report by the Secretariat," Fifty-Second World Health Assembly, provisional agenda item, April 15, 1999, online at http://ftp.who.int/gb/archive/pdf_files/WHA52/ew5.pdf.

Gone! This example illustrates Western thinking toward gaining knowledge for improving physical health. (It also highlights the importance of ethical considerations when conducting research; James Phipps was lucky that Jenner was right!)

Medicine continued to progress, marked by key findings that served to form a solid foundation for effective diagnoses and treatment of medical illness. The list below highlights some accomplishments of medical science since the late 1800s.

- X-rays to image bone and tissues have been discovered.
- Marie Curie initiated research on "uranium waves," which led to the discovery of radioactivity. Radiation is commonly used in the diagnoses and treatment of physical illness.[5]
- Life expectancy has nearly doubled in the twentieth century as a result of improved medical techniques and more sanitary living conditions.
- Several diseases have been eliminated through the development of vaccinations.
- Improved medicines have been developed since the establishment of molecular biology.
- Insulin has been discovered and used to treat diabetes.
- The antibiotic penicillin has been discovered and used to treat infections.
- Open heart surgery has been developed and advanced.
- Inhalers have been developed to alleviate the symptoms of asthma.

---

5. Naomi Pasachoff, *Marie Curie and the Science of Radioactivity* (New York and Oxford: Oxford University Press, 1996). Available online at American Institute of Physics, 2000, http://www.aip.org/history/curie unstable.htm.

- The CAT (Computerized Axial Tomography) scan has been developed to show a picture of cross sections through parts of the body.
- The human genome has been mapped and will encourage new understanding and treatment of diseases.[6]

The scientific method has yielded an abundance of fruitful findings in the natural sciences. Louis Pasteur discovered how microorganisms could contaminate milk. He developed a process to heat the liquid and destroy the harmful bacteria. The procedure is called pasteurization to honor the scientist who developed the practice. Evangelista Torricelli's invention of the barometer, Alexander Graham Bell's design of the telephone, and Guglielmo Marconi's development of the radio all serve as practical examples of ways that science is able to improve our lives.

With the physical sciences making important tangible developments it is little wonder that psychologists looked on with envy. The philosophical and psychological arenas, by their very natures, are simply not as scientific as the natural sciences. Explaining *why* a nine-year-old stole an apple from a street vendor is more challenging than describing the fractured radius (bone below the elbow) the same boy received when being pursued by the irate merchant. Furthermore, casting the young lad's bone is easier than "fixing" his potential inclination toward thievery.

Fallen Analogy

This is not to say the scientific study of mental health is not a legitimate and important discipline. This field of study has made significant contributions to understanding how the mind

6. Association of the British Pharmaceutical Industry, "History of Medicine Timeline," Resources for Schools, 2007, http://www.abpischools.org.uk/res/coResourceImport/resources04/history/timeline.cfm.

works. Child development, family counseling, and substance abuse treatment are a few areas that have benefited from rigid examination of mental and behavioral functioning. However, the direct analogy between medical science and psychology is misguided. The field of psychology, by its own admission, operates from many different and often contrasting theoretical frameworks and treatment approaches.

There has been much confusion within the mental health field. For almost any general psychological theory there is another that is in direct opposition. By itself that is not necessarily a bad thing because theories are educated guesses. Many theories can be tested scientifically to reveal data either supportive or not supportive of the assumptions made. However, the mental health field has a history of working from leading *theories* as if they were established, scientifically proven *facts*. In its effort to match the respectability of medicine and the other hard sciences, psychology has forcefully embraced the exclusive use of the scientific method and discarded wisdom literature (religious, philosophical, and cultural belief systems) as *the* way to understand the multi-dimensional human psyche. This approach has confounded the field as often as it has led to progress.

To make matters more baffling, the majority of psychology's most influential writers have taken it upon themselves to demonize religious and spiritual convictions that lead to the formation of character. From psychology's inception many prominent writers in the field have labeled believers irrational, obsessed, or mentally disturbed. The word *psychotherapy* literally means "care of the soul," but the spiritual element of humanity has been severed by prominent theorists in the mental health field. The result has been slower development of an alliance of faith and reason as a way to understand human behaviors and enhance overall wellness.

Perhaps the most striking irony found in the discipline of psychology is that its founders and lead theorists have aggressively attacked religion in general and Christianity in particular, even in a society with strong religious underpinnings. Faith and values, which are embraced by that majority of United States citizens, have been deemed either meaningless or harmful by virtually all key psychological theorists. Our nation has a strong tradition of values and beliefs, dating back to the founding fathers. Fully 96 percent of the population believes that God exists. Another 80 percent would say that they are "convinced" of this reality. Compare this to the 5 percent who believe that God "does not exist," and 1 percent who make such a claim with certainty.[7]

One reason for this dichotomy is that as individuals obtain higher levels of education they tend to be less religious. This may explain some of the disparity among mental health professionals and the general population. A 1990 national poll of psychotherapists found that mental health professionals had a higher prevalence of agnosticism and atheism than the average American.[8]

MENTAL HEALTH PROFESSIONAL
PERCENT OF ATHEISM/AGNOSTICISM

Clinical Psychologists	28
Psychiatrists	21
Clinical Social Workers	9
Marriage and Family Therapists	7

7. David Masci and Gregory A. Smith, "God is Alive and Well in America," Pew Forum on Religion and Public Life (Washington, D.C.: PewResearchCenter Publications), April 4, 2006, http://pewresearch.org/pubs/15/god-is-alive-and-well-in-America.

8. Allen E. Bergin and Jay P. Jensen, "Religiosity of Psychotherapists: A National Survey," *Psychotherapy: Theory, Research, Practice Training* 27, no. 1 (1990): 3–7.

A 2007 study examining faith beliefs among psychologists in the United States posted similar findings.[9] Psychologists were three times more likely than the general public to dismiss religion as irrelevant to life, and they were five times more likely to describe themselves as atheist or agnostic. In virtually every category assessed psychologists were far less religious than the clients they serve. Related research examining faith beliefs among medical doctors found psychiatrists to be the least religious among all physicians.[10]

While it is important to understand the established negative bias toward spirituality and the current disparity between service provider and client, it is equally important to acknowledge psychology's contributions. Many people who enter the profession do so with an altruistic motivation to serve others. Those who work in the field, especially below the rank of psychologist and psychiatrist, would be quick to admit that money is not the prime motivator. Instead, their goal is helping others achieve an improved quality of life.

These mental health service providers help clients in a variety of ways, and those with *less* education tend to spend more one-on-one time with patients. In outpatient mental health facilities psychiatrists tend to be more concerned with medication issues, often limited to between fifteen and thirty minutes with patients every month. Psychologists who work in similar facilities typically conduct periodic mental health evaluations and provide one-on-one treatment for approximately one hour on

9. Harold D. Delaney, William R. Miller, and Ana M. Bisono, "Religiosity and Spirituality among Psychologists: A Survey of Clinician Members of the American Psychological Association," *Professional Psychology: Research and Practice* 38, no. 5 (2007): 540.

10. Farr Culin, study author, "Psychiatrists are the least religious of all physicians," University of Chicago Medical Center, Sept. 3, 2007, http://www.uchospitals.edu/news/2007/20070903-psychiatrists.html.

a bi-weekly basis. Most programs that offer community mental health treatments employ therapists with masters or bachelors degrees to spend time with clients at least weekly. In residential treatment facilities paraprofessionals, who receive only behavioral management training, help residents succeed with daily program requirements.

WORLDVIEW

"Where there is no vision, the people perish."
— Proverbs 29:18 (KJV)

One of the more discouraging parts of my job as a "mobile therapist" was my work with troubled teenagers, who had already received years of community mental health treatment dating back to their childhood days. We usually visited during weekly hour-long office therapy sessions, or longer weekly home-based counseling sessions. Psychological assessments and psychiatric visits to assess medication needs were part of the standard regimen. It was not unusual for these youth to periodically require inpatient services lasting weeks to months at regional mental health facilities. Yet in spite of much professional mental health attention, these teens had not been exposed to religious or spiritual practices or taught virtues. Character traits such as persistence, humility, and gratitude were missing from their lives. The teens would not be taught about such characteristics in counseling because traditional mental health has labeled such teaching archaic and unscientific. With the desire for "scientific" answers and the rejection of values as part of implementing change, we overlook potential solutions.

While standard mental health services can help these youngsters and their families, the saturation of services also gives teens an extra hurdle to jump by labeling them with a mental illness. One of the ironies I have experienced in my work is the contradictory nature seen in the youth around mid to late teenage years. Typically during counseling sessions they will behave in a polite manner, as most parents would expect from their own children. Ultimately we would talk about their troubled thoughts and behaviors at home, in school, or in the community. The too common and seemingly genuine response has been, "I can't help it. I've got a mental problem." These teens—who do not receive teaching on values to help overcome obstacles and who view their mental health problem as a medical issue—do not understand their own role in behavior changes or overall mental wellness.

Worldview. Outlook. Paradigm. Attitude. Habits. Role. Reason. Purpose. We can choose our own descriptions, but what we believe about life largely determines the way we live. The older kids I have worked with have experiences that speak to a field that has discarded centuries of established wisdom. In the next several chapters we will explore classical theorists and their influence on the discipline of psychology as well as the four major perspectives in the field. Later we will see how psychotherapy is hopefully beginning to find some solid footing.

2

Faith in Reason

*"One learns through the heart,
not the eyes or the intellect."*[1]

—MARK TWAIN

*"The madman is not the man who has lost his reason.
The madman is the man who has lost everything
except his reason."*[2]

—G. K. CHESTERTON

A BRIEF trip back into time will help us see where the field of psychology is today. We saw in the previous chapter that since psychology's development there has been a desire to establish it as a science, just like its brothers in the natural or hard sciences. One method of gaining acceptance into the family has been to distance itself from the "soft" field of philosophy. Values, beliefs, and words of wisdom would have no place in the sophisticated, statistically cultured world of mind and behavior. Over time this tendency to view mental health as distinct from

---

1. Mark Twain, "What Paul Bourget Thinks of Us." Available online at www.fullbooks.com/Essays-on-Paul Bourget.html.

2. G. K. Chesterton, *Orthodoxy* (John Lane Co., 1908), chapter 2. Available online at http://www.geocities.com/charles_glenn/orthodox.htm.

body and soul has taken root and certainly is the tone in most contemporary scholarly pursuits and practice within the field.

The desire of psychologists to be removed from philosophers and to become "scientific" like the hard sciences was not always so intense. In fact, until the nineteenth century psychology was a branch of philosophy. Wilhelm Wundt, who is credited with founding modern experimental psychology, established the first laboratory devoted solely to the study of psychological research at Leipzig, Germany, in 1876. He viewed his own work as an extension of philosophy. In essence, his goal was to apply the scientific method to address philosophical questions related to mental functioning, such as the origin of feelings, thoughts, and ideas.[3]

William James (1842–1910), considered to be the "father of American psychology," was a prolific writer, and he greatly helped to advance the understanding of psychological principles. In 1890 his 1200-page masterpiece, *The Principles of Psychology*, laid a foundation for continuing development in the field. A key purpose of his work was to describe foundational precepts established at that time, including the function of the brain's hemispheres, cerebral blood supply, stream of thought, memory, and ability make sense of the self.

James also discusses the soul and spiritual self as fundamentals that are to be considered within psychology, but he intentionally and almost timidly places this discussion of the soul after a medical-like description regarding the working of the mind. He is careful to address those who are "anti-spiritualistic," favoring a view of the mind limited to organic chemical

---

3. Thomas, Nigel J.T., "Mental Imagery," supplement "Founders of Experimental Psychology: Wilhelm Wundt and William James," *The Stanford Encyclopedia of Philosophy* (Fall 2008 Edition), Edward N. Zalta (ed.), forthcoming URL = <http://plato.stanford.edu/archives/fall2008/entries/mental-imagery/>.

functioning. When elaborating on the "soul-theory" he speaks in place of the reader and asks, "Why on earth doesn't the poor man say *the soul* and have done with it?" He answers his own question when writing that "my only reason for beating the bushes so…[is that] I might perhaps force some of these materialistic minds to feel the more strongly the logical respectability of the spiritualistic position. The fact is that one cannot afford to despise any of these great traditional objects of belief."[4]

James was certainly interested in religion. Many of his works concerned the feasibility of studying how faith impacts a person's life. In *The Varieties of Religious Experience* James explores human nature that relates to the divine. According to James, happy and healthy-minded religious people may have a natural disposition with which they are born, but more likely such a character trait is the result of the will. These individuals choose to see the good in life, even when life hands them difficulties. Individuals with this mindset seem to have the habit of "flinging themselves upon their sense of the goodness of life, in spite of the hardships of their own condition."[5]

James gives contrast to this state of mind by describing the "Sick Soul" as a person who experiences a simmering sense of gloom. He suggests that some with this inclination will never heal, while others can overcome this tendency. James goes on to discuss well-known evangelists, highlighting the serenity of their lives, often amid painful circumstances. He says that they reach a state marked by the "loss of all the worry, the sense that all is ultimately well with one, the peace, the harmony, the *willingness*

---

4. William James, *The Principles of Psychology*, vol. 1 (1890; NY: Dover Publications, Inc., 1950), 181. Citations are to the Dover edition.

5. William James, *The Varieties of Religious Experience: A Study in Human Nature* (New York: Random House, 1902), 78.

to be, even though the outer conditions should remain the same" (emphasis added by author).⁶

Unlike future psychologists, James saw spiritual and religious experiences as a valuable component of the human condition. However, he took the position that because such beliefs unite us with a divine nature this type of experience is not available to customary methods of scientific research. James did not view the relationship between faith and mental health with antagonism. In fact, he suggested that all faiths have value if that particular belief is helpful to an individual. He believed that faith unites us with a Higher Force and can offer a profound sense of meaning and purpose in life. He writes, "God is the natural appellation (name), for us Christians at least, for the supreme reality, so I will call this higher part of the universe by the name of God. We and God have business with each other; and in opening ourselves to his influence our deepest destiny is fulfilled."⁷

"Whoever it was who searched the heavens with his telescope and could find no God, would not have found the human mind if he had searched the brain with a microscope."⁸

—George Santayana

James's openness to the value of faith was unusual and short lived in psychology. It was not long before early thinkers began to influence the field by instilling their particular brand

6. Ibid., 242.

7. Ibid., 507.

8. George Santayana, *The Life of Reason*; or *The Phases of Human Progress* in 5 volumes, (New York: Charles Scribner's Sons, 1905), reprinted George Santayana, *The Life of Reason*, vol. 1 (New York: Dover Publications, Inc., 1980). Dover edition available online at Bored. com, ebooks, 2008, www.bored.com/ebooks/Philosophy/american/life%20of%20reason.html.

of religion—humanism—into psychology as a discipline. The first person to receive a Ph.D. in psychology was G. Stanley Hall (1844-1924). He studied under William James and set an example for others—one they certainly followed. Hall had a dramatic and antagonistic view of the relationship between psychology and faith. Where James held an open, practical view of religion, Hall wished to establish what could be considered his own, new religion of psychology. He felt that scientific psychology should and would replace the need for religion.

Hall drew inspiration from religion, but he was not religious. While he greatly admired Jesus, he saw him as a peer, one he considered a prophet along with himself.[9] Humility may have not been one of G. Stanley's finer character strengths. In his 1923 book *Life and Confessions of a Psychologist*, written a year before his death, Hall wrote,

> I have become a riper product of the present stage of civilization than most of my contemporaries, have outgrown more superstitions, attained clearer insights, and have a deeper sense of peace with myself. I love but perhaps still more pity mankind, groping and stumbling, often slipping backward along the upward Path, which I believe I see just as clearly as Jesus or Buddha did, the two greatest souls that ever walked this earth and whom I supremely revere.[10]

Hall did not proclaim to be divine, but did attempt to strip Jesus of his divinity though psychoanalysis. In his 1917 work *Jesus,*

---

9. Clarence J. Karier, "G. (1983) Stanley Hall: A Priestly Prophet of a New Dispensation." *Journal of Libertarian Studies* 7, no. 1 (Spring, 1983): 35–60.

10. G. Stanley Hall, *Life and Confessions of a Psychologist* (NY: Appleton and Co., 1923), 596.

the Christ, in the Light of Psychology, Hall wrote that "Man is the only divinity, or at least God is only a collective term for man."[11]

For G. Stanley, God as a supreme being did not exist. With no God, there is no need for religion. Yet much of mankind's philosophy and psychology has been heavily influenced by religious tenets. Hall felt that his new scientific psychology would close the gap between psychology and religion, simply by doing away with faith beliefs once and for all. He believed that only man is divine because life continues from generation to generation. He termed this type of anthropological immortality "Mansoul." For Hall, psychology would capture religion to the point where the most devout believers would be ashamed to hold onto thoughts opposed by and ultimately forbidden by the new "secular faith" of the mental health system.

Hall made a statement that set the tone for the relationship between psychology and religion, declaring, *"When psychology has expelled the last vestige of magic from religion and taken its place, then only shall we have a psychotherapy that is true to its name."*[12] In this new religion the priest is replaced by the psychologist, and sin is exchanged for sickness.

Hall's gospel spread! He founded the American Psychological Association, established a psychological laboratory at Johns Hopkins University, founded and served as the first president of Clark University, and started several journals, including the *American Journal of Psychology,* the *Journal of Religious Psychology,* and the *Journal of Applied Psychology.* He was a prolific writer on child and youth development and had a profound impact on American education. His desire to position psychol-

---

11. As cited in Clarence J. Karier, "G. Stanley Hall: A Priestly Prophet of a New Dispensation," *Journal of Libertarian Studies* 7, no. 1 (Spring 1983): 39.

12. Ibid., 45.

ogy as the new, scientific religion is embedded in the field. His followers would carry his standard for the next hundred years.

Since the time of G. Stanley Hall there have been four major types of treatment or psychotherapies used to help relieve mental and emotional distress. These perspectives about the workings of the human mind include[13]

1. Psychoanalysis—the belief that powerful inner forces, most buried in the unconscious mind, dictate behavior.
2. Behaviorism—the belief that observable behavior and environment, *not inner forces*, is the only way to understand a person's actions.
3. Humanism—the belief that behavior is a result of a person's untainted values and instinctive choices, more than his or her unconscious mind or environment.
4. Cognitive—the focus on how the mind *processes* information (similar to the way in which computers *process* data) through functions such as perception, memory, reasoning, and beliefs.

While there are a range of additional views that could be added to this list, these four have been most influential in developing our understanding of psychological wellness and how mental health treatment is approached.

---

13. David G. Myers, *Psychology*, 7th ed. (NY: Worth Publishers, 2004), 673.

3

In Freud We Trust?

"Ultimately faith is the only key to the universe. The final meaning of human existence, and the answers to questions on which all our happiness depends cannot be reached in any other way."[1]

—Thomas Merton

"I should add that I stand in no awe whatsoever of the Almighty. If we were ever to meet I should have more reproaches to make to Him than He could to me."[2]

—Sigmund Freud

Sigmund Freud is a big name in psychology's development. It would be difficult to overemphasize either the scholarly influence of Freud's work or the societal impact. He solidified and popularized a secular view of mental health. Perhaps best recognized as the father of psychoanalysis, Freud (1856–1939) believed humans functioned from their unconscious mind. His views have lead to mental health treatment primarily based on an illness model, with the focus on the pathology or problem and

1. Thomas Merton, *New Seeds of Contemplation* (Norfolk, CT: New Directions Book, 1961), 130. Thomas Merton, *New Seeds of Contemplation* (Norfolk, CT: New Directions Book, 1961), 130.

2. As cited in Ryan LaMothe, "Freud, Religion, and the Presence of Projective Identification, *Psychoanalytic Psychology* 20, no. 2 (Spring 2003): 298.

little attention directed to what may be effective and positive in a person's life. Countless articles and books have been devoted to understanding and interpreting exactly what Freud meant in many of his writings. In academic writings and therapeutic practice, Freud's ideas continue to evoke heated response—some supporting and others condemning his views.

FREUD'S THEORIES

Arguably Freud's most famous speculation is termed the Oedipal crisis. The Oedipal crisis is the third stage in Freud's developmental theory, occurring around the age of 5.[3] During this stage a child has an exclusive, incestual love for the opposite sex parent and an unconscious desire for the death of the same sex parent. In the case of a boy he would wish to kill his father and sleep with his mother because of his sexual attraction to her. The boy also has what Freud calls "castration anxiety," which is the fear that he will lose his penis. Part of this fear is the result of the rivalry the boy feels from his father over the love of his mother. Eventually the boy moves through this stage by deferring to his bigger, stronger, dominant dad, and he sets his sights from his mom to girls, and eventually to women. At this point the boy accepts his dad and strives to become a guy just like him. "Siggie" (the nickname Freud's mother gave him) selected the term *Oedipus* based on the Greek legend of the king who killed his father and inadvertently married his mother.

Girls, on the other hand, wish to kill their mother and sleep with their father because of penis envy, which is a female's desire to have male reproductive organs. Freud's logic is that girls notice the physical differences between females and males and feel cheated of the power associated with manhood. Girls

3. Freud, Sigmund, *New Introductory Lectures on Psychoanalysis* (NY: W. W. Norton and Co., 1965), 1–12.

wish they had a penis and want to have at least some type of substitute, such as a child of their own. The daughter desires her father, but she eventually acknowledges that he is already taken. Finally she accepts reality, identifies with her mother, and adjusts her sights to boys and then to finding a man of her own. Freud tells us that this crisis leads to assimilation with the same-sex parent and the development of the superego. The superego can be described as a person's acceptance of society's morals and the development of the conscious.

It is difficult to describe these theories (and read about them) without feeling uncomfortable, to say the least. This theory implies that a host of negative and even hateful thoughts exist between what ought to be extremely close family members. Simply stated, these thoughts are repulsive, but giving such an honest evaluation will bring severe criticism from many who have been schooled in psychology. We must ask where Freud came up with these scientific discoveries. Was it through experimental research or the collection and analysis of hard data? No. Instead he arrived at these theories primarily through case histories of the troubled behavior of his patients and *his own self-analysis*—his detached observations about himself and his past. Therapists can certainly learn a great deal about human nature and behavior through their work of trying to alleviate emotional distress. However, to extrapolate the experience of people who show signs of unusual behavior as a universal developmental stage is simply not scientific.

Peter Muris writes in the *Journal of Child and Family Studies* that "Freud's theory is largely based on case studies of abnormal human behavior. Without exceptions, these cases are fascinating and interesting. However, from a scientific point of view, Freud's analyses of these cases are unacceptable, as the main concepts of his theory cannot be validated empirically."[4]

4. Peter Muris, "Freud Was Right . . . about the Origins of Abnormal

In addition to case studies, Freud drew upon his personal reflections as a child. In a letter to a friend, Wilhelm Fliess, he states,

> I have found, in my own case too, [the phenomenon of] being in love with my mother and jealous of my father, and I now consider it a universal event in early childhood, even if not so early as in children who have been made hysterical.[5]

Herein lays a key problem with foundational "scientific" psychology. This theory cannot be tested or examined in a true scientific manner. It is basically analytical insights about oneself. To suggest that this experience is a "universal event" is not only baseless, but it serves to strip humanity of its dignity.

At the time of this writing my three youngest children are twelve, nine, and six years old. As most parents do, I understand my children to be a gift and blessing. As I see them grow in their innocence, laughing and playing childlike, there is no hint of the twisted developmental events put forth in Oedipus. It is regrettable that this theory has helped to shape the mental landscape of our society in the name of "science."

Freud, like virtually all of the key pioneers in the field, was able to develop these theories only after rejecting the existence of a Supreme Being. With human beings ascending to supremacy within the universe, faith beliefs would now be properly understood as a sign of illness, an inability to deal with the world. In Freud's view religion

---

Behavior," *Journal of Child and Family Studies* 15, no. 1 (2006): 1–12.

5. Jean Chiriac, "Sigmund Freud's Self-Analysis," as cited from October 15, 1897, Masson, J. M. ed., "The complete letters of Sigmund Freud to Wilhelm Fliess," 1887–1904 (Cambridge: Harvard University Press, 1985). Available online at http://www.freudfile.org/self_analysis_continue.html.

> consists in depressing the value of life and distorting the picture of the real world in a delusional manner—which presupposes an intimidation of the intelligence. At this price, by forcibly fixing them [religious believers] in a state of psychical infantilism and by drawing them into a mass-delusion, religion succeeds in sparing many people an individual neurosis. But hardly anything more (author addition in brackets).[6]

In his book *The Future of an Illusion* Freud details his belief that science is the only way to understand the world and our place in it. Religion is, as the title of his book reflects, nothing more than an illusion. Religious principles are mere fantasy. When discussing tenets of faith he writes,

> We can now repeat that all of them are illusions and insusceptible of proof. No one can be compelled to think them true, to believe in them. Some of them are so improbable, so incompatible with everything we have laboriously discovered about the reality of the world, that we may compare them—if we pay proper regard to the psychological differences—to delusions.[7]

Ironically, while Freud gleans great insights from case studies and his own experiences, such ways of learning are deemed irrelevant when faith is involved. He writes, "Scientific work is the only road which can lead us to a knowledge of reality outside ourselves. It is once again merely an illusion to expect anything from intuition and introspection."[8]

6. Sigmund Freud, *Civilization and Its Discontents* (NY: W. W. Norton and Co., 1961), 31–32.

7. Sigmund Freud, *The Future of an Illusion* (NY: W. W. Norton and Co., 1961), 31.

8. Ibid.

FREUD'S INFLUENCE ON CURRENT TREATMENT

His development of the psychoanalytic approach to mental health is no longer the dominant view in clinical psychology, but it continues to be widely utilized through forms of "talk therapy." His cultural impact is evident. Our vocabulary is seasoned with his terminology: ego, repression, disorders, the unconscious, neurotic, psychotic, and denial. Even the term *Freudian slip* is understood as an individual's misstatement or mistake caused by the unconscious mind.

Few scholars or mental health practitioners currently embrace all of Freud's theories about the workings of the human mind. Today, as in the past, there are Freudian scholars who debate what was actually meant by Oedipus and other theories he put forth. This is appropriate as Freud is certainly credited with helping advance knowledge about mental health, especially regarding the importance of child development. However, in a discipline splintered by combative presumptions, there is reluctance to dispel even his most outrageous theories as absurd.

No matter how worn, the field of psychology embraces founding theories. This does not happen, or at least happens much less, in the natural sciences. In the Middle Ages bleeding was a technique used to reduce fever in a patient. Individuals often received too much "treatment," resulting in their death. While this treatment has been deemed archaic and replaced by a host of advancements, psychology has been reluctant to move forward and replace old theories and treatments.

Meanwhile, many mental health patients accept as fact any theory presented as "established." In Freud's case, the point is not to attack the man, his efforts, or his theories. He certainly had valuable insights that have been built upon to further understand the workings of the mind. However, his unhealthy views of humanity seep into society. The unspeakable joy of a daughter's hug and good night kiss is poisoned with toxic sexual overtones. Children are seen as animalistic, stripped of their natural innocence and childlike purity.

One of the ironies of Freud's impact upon the "scientific" field of psychology is that his work is blatantly non-scientific. Many of his ideas, such as the Oedipal concept, are plainly odd as well as not testable. His more reasonable ideas about inner forces and the unconscious mind have some validity to them (and many have been shown to be compelling, such as the importance of childhood and development), but they still do not readily lend themselves to rigid analysis. It was largely for this reason that a competing school of thought, behavioralism, evolved as a major force in psychology.

> *"If a person only learns and accepts what the intellect can grasp, it will eventually and positively prohibit the person from progressing on the mystical path."*[9]
>
> —STEPHEN J. ROSSI

> *"A religious agency is a special form of government under which 'good' and 'bad' become 'pious' and 'sinful.'"*[10]
>
> —B. F. SKINNER

BEHAVIORAL "SCIENTIFIC" VIEWS

Behavioralists believe that people are born with a mind completely impressionable and that behaviors are determined entirely by an individual's environment and circumstances. This view

---

9. Stephen J. Rossi, *When the Lion Roars: A Primer for the Unsuspecting Mystic* (Notre Dame, IN: Ava Maria Press, 2003), 102.

10. B. F. Skinner, *Beyond Freedom and Dignity* (New York: Alfred A. Knopf, 1971), 116.

of human nature dates back to the time of the philosopher John Locke (1632–1704), who described the mind as a *tabula rasa,* or blank slate. Behavioralists make a clear distinction between thought and behavior. Behaviors can be observed, and therefore measured, while thoughts cannot. Behavioralists contend that since behaviors can be observed they can then be methodically, scientifically examined, as opposed to the vague, introspective approach of psychoanalysis.

One of the more well-known pioneers in this field is the Russian physicist Ivan Pavlov (1849–1936), who conducted his famous classical conditioning experiment with dogs. In this experiment Pavlov would repeatedly feed his dogs and ring a bell at the same time. The animals' mouth would salivate in anticipation of the meal. After a period of time Pavlov would sound the bell *without* feeding the dogs, and he observed that the animals would still drool because they had been conditioned to associate the sound of the bell with food. This experiment demonstrated how conditioning is part of the learning process in which a response (saliva) becomes related to a new stimulus (sound of the bell).

Behavioral psychologists approached humanity from this same perspective. Again with a strong desire to be as objective as the physical sciences, their worldview was one in which mankind was primarily seen as animalistic. John B. Watson, an early behavioralist psychologist, makes this view plain when writing,

> Behaviorists believe that there is nothing from within to develop. If you start with a healthy body, the right number of fingers and toes, eyes, and the few elementary movements that are present at birth, you do not need anything else in the way of raw material to make a man, be that man a genius, a cultured gentleman, a rowdy or a thug.[11]

11. John B. Watson, *Psychological Care of Infant and Child* (New York:

The most famous and influential behaviorialist, B. F. Skinner (1904–1990), also believed humans function essentially the same way as animals. Skinner completely rejected the idea that people had free will, with values and beliefs that could guide their lives. Instead he was convinced that individuals are controlled entirely by stimulus within their environments, essentially negating the possibility of innate freedom. Skinner was clear in his beliefs and wrote, "The hypothesis that man is not free is essential to the application of scientific method to the study of human behavior."[12] Skinner believed that character, values, faith, freedom, and dignity should have no place in psychology, or in the understanding of mankind.

Skinner's thinking is rather chilling. His would be a world of social engineering where there are those who control individuals and those controlled by the elites. In his book *Beyond Freedom and Dignity* he states that a person "plays two roles: one as a controller, as the designer of a controlling culture, and another as the controlled, as the products of a culture."[13] He arrives at this view by devaluing humanity to the level of mortal slave.

Perhaps a more appropriate title for his work would have been *"Beneath" Freedom and Dignity*, in that Skinner unflinchingly proposes a view of human nature that strips individuals of autonomy and respect. Skinner suggests that we should simply surrender to the reality that no one has free will. All of our actions are determined for us by the environment in which we live. As for characteristics such as dignity, we should grow up. For Skinner, dignity is nothing more than a weak mental construct we have created to mask admirable behaviors or talents

---

W. W. Norton & Company, 1928), 87.

12. B. F. Skinner, *Science and Human Behavior* (New York: Macmillan, 1953), 447.

13. B. F. Skinner, *Beyond Freedom and Dignity* (New York: Alfred A. Knopf, 1971), 197.

in people that can't be explained scientifically. He believed the inspiration most see in the courage of a firefighter, the devotion of inner-city school teachers, and the care of humanitarian relief workers is not accounted for by science. In refuting the notion of dignity, Skinner writes, "As for admiration in the sense of wonderment, the behavior we admire is the behavior we cannot yet explain. Science naturally seeks a fuller explanation of that behavior; its goal is the destruction of mystery."[14]

To pure behavioralists there exists no mystery or awe in life. All of human conduct can be accounted for by stimulus-response, reward-punishment. Humanity equates with animality. Skinner argues that the "traditional" view of man having freedom, dignity, and living a life guided by values must be done away with. Only then can we see people for what they really are—animals. Explaining the urgent need to shift from a holistic view of man to a strictly corporal one he writes,

> It is often said that in doing so we must treat the man who survives as a mere animal. "Animal" is a pejorative term, but only because "man" has been made spuriously honorific. Krutch has argued that whereas the traditional view supports Hamlet's exclamation, "How like a god!" Pavlov, the behavioral scientist, emphasized "How like a dog!" But that was a step forward. A god is the archetypal pattern of an explanatory fiction, of a miracle-working mind, of the metaphysical. Man is much more than a dog, but like a dog he is within range of scientific analysis.[15]

Skinner's endorsement of man "like a dog" did not gain the momentum he had hoped for within the discipline. While the psychoanalytic and behavioralist views of human nature (known

14. Ibid., 58.
15. Ibid., 201.

as the "first" and "second" force in psychology) dominated thinking well into the twenty-first century, it became evident that the field verged on militant secularism. By demonizing religion and faith beliefs, key thinkers had also discarded common, universally desirable values such as love, beauty, peace, strength, joy, truth, and goodness. These and similar virtues championed by the world's great religions for thousands of years were now relegated to the mythical realm of faith, beyond the scope and interest of most psychologists.

4

Is Life All about Me?

*"We cannot live only for ourselves. A thousand fibers
connect us with our fellow-men;
and along those fibers, as sympathetic threads,
our actions run as causes, and they come back
to us as effects."*[1]

—HERMAN MELVILLE

*"Neither the Bible nor the prophets; neither Freud nor research;
neither the revelation of God nor Man; can take precedence over my
own direct experience."*[2]

—CARL ROGERS

HUMANIST PSYCHOLOGY would evolve as the third force within the discipline since it offered those seeking to understand people an alternative to psychoanalysis or behavioralism. Humanists believe that individuals are controlled by their own values more than by the environment or their subconscious minds. This approach to understanding mental health is a welcome change, as it at least begins to move in a more positive

---

1. As cited in Laurence G. Boldt, *Zen Soup: Tasty Morsels of Wisdom from Great Minds East and West* (New York: Penguin Group, 1997), 142.

2. Carl R. Rogers, *On Becoming a Person* (Boston: Houghton Mifflin, 1961), 24.

direction toward wellness. The two most famous thinkers in this area are Abraham Maslow and Carl Rogers.

HUMANIST THEORISTS

Maslow (1908–1970) may be most famous for his "hierarchy of needs," often depicted as a five-layer pyramid anchored by basic physical needs such as food and shelter and peaking at self-actualization, where individuals are able to practice creativity, solve life's problems, and live a moral life. Unlike most of his predecessors in psychology, he was open to the possibility of spirituality and values influencing life. He was also out of step with his peers because he studied psychology by examining individuals who exemplified mental health, rather than those with severe emotional problems. Maslow discovered that mentally strong individuals shared certain traits—traits that could be seen as examples of wellness. He was a proponent of spiritual experiences and values, but as a lifelong atheist he was not a supporter of organized religion. Maslow advocated for an individualized spirituality, uncluttered by organized religion and belief in a Supreme Being. In his book *Religion, Values, and Peak Experiences* he makes the point that writing about the terms *spirituality* and *religion* is difficult for a psychologist.

> It is almost impossible to speak of the "spiritual life" (a distasteful phrase to a scientist, and especially to a psychologist) without using the vocabulary of traditional religion....This makes an almost insoluble problem for the writer who is intent on demonstrating that the common base of all religion is human, natural, empirical, and that so-called spiritual values are also naturally derivable. But I have only theistic language available for this "scientific" job.[3]

3. Abraham H. Maslow, *Religions, Values, and Peak Experiences* (New York: Viking Press, 1964), 4.

Maslow is to be credited with encouraging a dialogue between science and religion, stressing the point that both ways of knowing have been mistakenly dichotomized. He displays humility when acknowledging that science has "become too exclusively mechanistic, too positivistic, too reductionistic, too desperately attempting to be value-free."[4] He cautions,

> Such an attitude dooms science to be nothing more than technology, amoral and non-ethical (as the Nazi doctors taught us). Such a science can be no more than a collection of instrumentalities, methods, techniques, nothing but a tool to be used by any man, good or evil, and for any ends, good or evil.[5]

Maslow certainly believed that "higher values," such as loving, accepting responsibility, and discovering meaning in life, played a critical role in good mental health. However, he also believed that such virtues could be accounted for at the human level, without the need for supernatural enlightenment. He proposed studying transcendent "peak-experiences" through the use of psychedelic drugs (such as LSD) to induce what he believed to be religious-like experiences.

Carl Rogers shared with Maslow credit for the development of humanistic psychology. Interestingly, Rogers (1902–1987) was raised with Christian beliefs and spent two years at Union Theological Seminary. It was during this time that he and some of his fellow students lost interest in religious studies, and he switched to the study of psychology. His interest was in questions

4, Ibid., 11.
5. Ibid., 12.

about the meaning of life, but he would not embrace Christian doctrine and teachings.[6]

Rogers's approach to mental health treatment seems quite innocuous, with many of his tenets sharing common ground with religious principles. He may be best known for the development of "client-centered" therapy. This form of treatment is anchored by Rogers's belief that human beings are intrinsically good and that people have unlimited potential for growth. Because people are basically good they have a natural tendency to move or grow toward "goodness." Understanding this natural positive leaning as being elemental to the human condition, the therapist's job is then to simply guide each client in search of life circumstances that are meaningful for him or her.

Left to our own devises we would naturally think and behave in a healthy manner. According to Rogers, people get off track when they try to meet the demands society places upon them in order to feel worthy. Rogers defines society as parents, school teachers, friends, classmates, and people with a close relationship to the client. He argues that children only receive rewards for being "good enough." Parents give children dessert when they finish their meals; school teachers give students a good grade for studying; classmates invite others to a party because they approve of those individuals' behaviors.

Rogers calls these rewards "conditional positive regard" because people receive positive feedback as a result of artificial conditioning, as opposed to natural behavioral desires. He feels individuals should be treated with *unconditional* positive regard to encourage people to function at their highest levels—similar to Maslow's concept of the "self-actualized" person. Rogers describes three key characteristics that mark his therapy and enable

---

6. Carl R. Rogers, *On Becoming a Person* (Boston: Houghton Mifflin, 1961), 8.

people to live the good life as "fully functioning" human beings. These are

1. First, an increasing openness to experience. This means being aware of external circumstances as they occur in life, as well as our internal response to those experiences, and accepting those responses or emotions.

2. Secondly, increasingly existential living. This entails bringing into each moment the realization that this experience has never been and will never come again. This understanding gives mature persons the ability to live fluid lives, unrestrained by rigid, preconceived expectations of what an experience should be.

3. And lastly, an increasing trust in himself. This is the idea that people should do what feels right as opposed to relying on a given set of principles, code of conduct, or expectations of others.

The first two principles are sensible, and at surface level align with many of the teachings of the world's great religions. Being aware of our feelings, both positive and negative, helps us to live well, as opposed to denying natural emotions, which leads to distress. Existential living is also understood as living "in the moment." People who live this way are said to live gracefully, being present in each moment and unattached to worries and pleasures of yesterday or tomorrow.

Rogers's third characteristic he calls "organismic trusting." This is the proverbial wolf in sheep's clothing. Organismic trusting is trusting oneself to behave in the most fulfilling manner in each circumstance. However, the key emphasis placed here (and throughout his writings) is *self*. Rogers, believing in the inherent goodness of each person, places each individual as the highest authority regarding behavior, which prompts clients to trust thoughts, instincts, and desires, wherever they lead.

If something feels right, good, or natural, go ahead and do it. Principles, values, parents, teachers, and preachers are seen as obstacles to satisfying the self. In his own explanation of organismic trusting he writes,

> In choosing what course of action to take in any situation, many people rely upon guiding principles, upon a code of action laid down by some group or institution . . . individuals are able to trust their total organismic reaction to a new situation because they discover to an ever-increasing degree that if they are open to their experience, doing what "feels right" proves to be a competent and trustworthy guide to behavior which is truly satisfying.[7]

Rogers exchanges the religious belief that guilt is a natural consequence of misbehavior for the accusation that pointless societal values are wrongly forced upon us as children. Since he believes that both children and adults will learn to self-regulate their behaviors naturally, individual guilt and conscience are abandoned in favor of childish—not childlike—freedoms. If you *feel* like having an affair and it works for you, that is great; if you *want* to cheat on a college exam or term paper and think you won't get caught, go for it; if someone makes you angry and you would *like* to take revenge, have at it. Morals and principles are relative to individuals. There are no universal truths, no guiding virtues. Instead, my reality is mine, and yours is yours. Rogers sums up this philosophy: "It appears to me that the way of the future must be to base our lives and our education on the assumption that there are as many realities as there are persons, and that our highest priority is to accept that hypothesis and proceed from there."[8]

---

7. Ibid., 189.

8. Excerpt from *The Carl Rogers Reader,* "A Philosophy of Persons,"

HUMANISTIC INFLUENCE IN SOCIETY

Rogers's beliefs continue to heavily influence the practice of psychology. He can be credited with moving the field beyond the Freudian, mechanistic "fix" mentality toward the acknowledgement that counselors can only support and guide those who wish to be well. At the same time his creed of "unconditional positive regard" has helped to cement a values-free atmosphere, where the only right or wrong in life is *not* following our every impulse. Character lessons from parents, coaches, religious or civic leaders are considered to impinge upon who we really are, which will be discovered once we remove all inhibitions. Morals and virtues, like religions, are archaic and meaningless constructs misguiding the uneducated masses.

Many counselors and therapists continue to take a Rogerian approach in their work. This is understandable for two key reasons. First, we live in a culture that promotes overindulgence and excess. Super-sized value meals, larger homes with smaller families, and cable or satellite television with hundreds of channels are among the more obvious signs of glut. If eating a second serving of fries while surfing hundreds of television channels on one of four plasma screens seems tempting, then it must be a good thing. The second reason is that human nature is susceptible to pride. We will happily accept guidance that excuses us from accountability. We cannot be held responsible when there is no ideal, no standard, or no one to be accountable to. We have become our own gods.

"All sin starts with the assumption that my false self, the self that exists only in my egocentric desires, is the fundamental reality of life

---

(Boston: Houghton Mifflin Company, 1989), as cited in Peace Meme, Longer Peaces, Dec. 12, 2006, http://peacememe.typepad.com/longer_peaces/2006/12/gold_from_carl_.html.

to which everything else in the universe is ordered."[9]

—THOMAS MERTON

"The concept of sin is the direct and indirect cause of virtually all neurotic disturbance. The sooner psychotherapists forthrightly begin to attack it the better their patients will be."[10]

—ALBERT ELLIS

COGNITIVE THEORISTS

While psychoanalysis, behaviorism, and humanism are considered to be the three major schools of thought in the development of modern psychology, one of the most recent and acclaimed approaches to mental health treatment is found in the cognitive view. Cognitive psychology has more of a common-sense feel to its approach than its predecessors. This view suggests that the way a person thinks or perceives a situation affects his or her emotions. Emotions influence the way we feel about life events, and they also impact our behaviors. Therefore, to change unwanted behaviors, we must be aware of how our thinking influences our emotions.

The grandfather of cognitive therapy is Albert Ellis (1913–2007). Ellis developed his particular brand of cognitive-behavioral therapy known as Rational-Emotive Therapy (RET), which later evolved into Rational Emotive Behavior Therapy

---

9. Thomas Merton, *New Seeds of Contemplation* (New York: New Directions, 1972), 34–35.

10. Albert Ellis, "There Is No Place for the Concept of Sin in Psychotherapy," *Journal of Counseling Psychology* 73, no. 3 (1960): 192.

(REBT).¹¹ REBT is a more direct form of treatment than its forerunners. Its basic tenet holds that it is not the circumstances in life that create mental distress, but a person's irrational interpretations or beliefs about those circumstances.

As an example let's imagine that you are from a small town and make a trip to the city. You stop to buy some coffee and realize you have no money because your pocket has been picked clean. This experience makes you angry and bitter towards city folk. REBT would counsel you to be rational and accept the reality that people with criminal inclination do exist and will steal when an opportunity presents itself. Accept that unfortunate—but real—truth and move on. Make behavioral adjustments, such as learning how to secure your money so that loss doesn't occur again. Unless you look at this situation rationally, you will not be able to effectively deal with the negative emotions of having your property taken and take the necessary actions to prevent such a loss in the future. Until you take such practical steps you'll be angry and bitter, unlikely to venture again into an urban setting.

Ellis, to his credit, was genuine and straightforward in his beliefs about human nature and the workings of the mind. He possessed an animated personality and may have been as famous for his salty language as for his contributions to the understanding of mental health. It was his view of mankind that largely influenced his *R* in "rational" emotive therapy. Ellis operated from a hedonistic worldview, believing that pleasure and the avoidance of pain are the ultimate goals of life. REBT is based on hedonism as a moral value. In *Reason and Emotion in Psychotherapy* Ellis states,

11. Albert Ellis, "Why Rational-Emotive Therapy to Rational Emotive Behavior Therapy?" *Psychotherapy: Theory, Research, Practice, Training* 36 no. 2 (Summer, 1999): 154–59.

> Just about all existing schools of psychology are, at bottom hedonistic, in that they hold that pleasure and freedom from pain are good and preferably should be the aims of thought and action. This is probably inevitable, because people who do not believe in a hedonistic view would continue to suffer intense anxiety and discomfort and would not come for therapy. And therapists who did not try in some manner to alleviate the discomfort of those who did come for help would hardly remain in business very long. Rational Emotive Behavior therapists, therefore, are far from unique when they accept some kind of hedonistic world view and try to help clients work for a hedonistic way of life.[12]

Ellis spent the early part of his career as a sexologist promoting a hedonist worldview in speeches and writing. Faithfulness, commitment, and self-restraint would be secondary to the satisfaction of the self. The titles of his books speak of his core beliefs. Among some of his revealing works are *Sex Without Guilt, Sex and the Liberated Man,* and *The Case for Promiscuity.* Ellis was a great proponent of self-indulgence as well as sexual freedoms. When lecturing college students he would encourage premarital sex, advocated open relationships for couples, and helped to legitimize sex apart from love and a committed relationship.

Ellis's contributions as a sexologist and his influence as a psychotherapist yield the same underlying lesson: the self reigns as queen or king. Life's purpose is to maximize pleasure and avoid pain, with the only caveat that your actions should not harm yourself or another. This view of man as god can only be proclaimed by one who has dethroned God—at least in his own mind. Ellis was not only an atheist, but for most of his career he

---

12. Albert Ellis, *Reason and Emotion in Psychotherapy,* rev. ed. (New York: Birch Lane Press Book, 1994), 292–293.

was a fervent opponent of religion. Religious beliefs marked by faith in a Supreme Being were signs of mental illness in his view, and he equated religion with masochism.

He would argue that those who believe in a Supreme Being are masochistic in that they intentionally deny the desires of the self, as seen in the Lenten fast rituals practiced by Christians or the self-denial during Ramadan by Muslims. Ellis made the case that even more than needless self-inhibition faith beliefs were a type of unhealthy compulsion that made it extremely difficult for the believer to be strong and autonomous. His worldview was rational, scientific, hedonistic, disdainful of spiritual possibilities. He writes,

> Devout, orthodox, or dogmatic religion (or what might be called religiosity) is significantly correlated with emotional disturbance . . . . The emotionally healthy individual is flexible, open, tolerant, and changing, and the devoutly religious person tends to be inflexible, closed, intolerant, and unchanging. Religiosity, therefore, is in many respects equivalent to irrational thinking and emotional disturbance.[13]

COGNITIVE INFLUENCE IN SOCIETY

REBT completely breaks with Freudian psychoanalysis in that the focus is on the here and now. You and I are responsible for our lives, not our mothers, fathers, sisters, and brothers. Ellis was not a fan of psychoanalysis, suggesting that "Freud was out of his (expletive) mind. He was as nutty as could be."[14] Cognitive

13. Albert Ellis, "Psychotherapy and Atheistic Values: A Response to A. E. Bergin's 'Psychotherapy and Religious Values,'" *Journal of Consulting and Clinical Psychology* 48, no. 5 (October 1980): 637.

14. Adam Green, "The Human Condition Ageless, Guiltless," *The New Yorker* magazine, October 13, 2003, http://www.newyorker.com

treatment to enhance mental wellness differs from Skinner's behavioralism in that it squarely places emotions and behaviors in the hands of the individual, rather than his or her environment. It is unlike Rogers's humanism in that unconditional trust in our feelings and instincts is replaced by examination of our thoughts and beliefs. Just because an emotion feels right, such as trusting in the inherent goodness of every city resident, does not mean that it is in our best interest.

Ellis, viewing the religious believer as mentally ill, does not call for neutrality in cognitive therapy, but instead he argues that faith beliefs are to be annihilated, replaced by a hedonistic, "rational" view of life. He urges counselors to pound away at unempirical religious thoughts and destroy the symptoms of emotional illness found in spiritual and religious practice. In his booklet aptly titled *The Case Against Religion* he writes,

> So will the therapist, if he himself is not too sick or gutless, attack his patient's religiosity. Not only will he show this patient that he is religious—meaning as we've previously noted, that he is masochistic, other-directed, intolerant, unable to accept uncertainty, unscientific, needlessly inhibited, self-abasing, and fanatic—but he will quite vigorously and forcefully question, challenge, and attack the patient's irrational beliefs that support these disturbed traits.[15]

Is psychotherapy value free? As Ellis said in a 2004 interview given to the *New York Times*, "While I'm alive, I want to keep

---

/archive/2003/10/13/031013ta_talk_green.

15. Albert Ellis, *The Case Against Religion: A Psychotherapist's View and the Case Against Religiosity* (Austin, TX: American Atheist Press, 1980), 16.

doing what I want to do. See people. Give workshops. Write, and preach the gospel according to St. Albert."[16]

In his later writings Albert Ellis would somewhat soften his rigid view that essentially equated religious beliefs with emotional disorder. Yet the vast majority of his work served to reinforce the antagonistic view of religion and spirituality held by most leading psychological theorists well into the twentieth century. The psychoanalytic and humanistic influences have filtered down through the psychological discipline and seeped into our culture.

Contemporary research now supports the notion that not only is counseling *not* value free, but that patient values tend to shift toward his or her therapist's values during the course of treatment.[17] The impact of these key thinkers has been profound. In 2003 the American Psychological Association honored Albert Ellis as the second most influential psychologist of the last century. The most influential psychologist of the twentieth century was Carl Rogers.[18]

---

16. Michael Kaufman, "Albert Ellis, 93, Influential Psychotherapist Dies," *The New York Times,* July 25, 2007, http://www.nytimes.com/2007/07/25/nyregion/25ellis.html?pagewanted=print.

17. Timothy A. Kelly and Hans H. Strupp, "Patient and Therapist Values in Psychotherapy: Perceived Changes, Assimilation, Similarity, and Outcome," *Journal of Consulting and Clinical Psychology* 60, no. 1 (February 1992): 34–40; Alan C. Tjeltveit, "The Good, the Bad, the Obligatory, and the Virtuous: The Ethical Contexts of Psychotherapy," *Journal of Psychotherapy Integration* 14, no. 2 (June 2004): 149–67.

18. Barry Farber, "Remembering Albert Ellis, a giant in American psychology—and a TC alum," Columbia University Teacher College, July 26, 2007, http://www.tc.columbia.edu/news/article.htm?id=6311.

5

Wheat and Weeds

*"'No,' he answered.
Because while you are pulling the weeds,
you may root up the wheat with them."*

—Matthew 13:29
New International Version

Now we come to a crossroad. As we have seen, psychology has made every effort to define itself as a genuine science that addresses natural phenomenon from an empirical, pragmatic, unbiased, and experimental fashion just like the natural sciences. Yet the leading theorists in the field defiantly violate the very principles of objectivity they profess to value. Freud's subliminal soul, Skinner's happy slave spirit, Rogers's theology of self, and St. Albert's hallowed hedonism were primarily, systematically, logically, scientifically extracted from the data analyses of their *beliefs?* Beliefs are ideas, personal convictions, and—here it comes—*faith*. All these theorists declared that faith in God, a Supreme Being, or Higher Power is irrelevant or a symptom of mental illness without hard data, empirical support, or *scientific findings* to support these claims.

While we might be tempted to dismiss the ideas of influential psychologists, let's pause for a moment. Though these theorists held secular, anti-religious views of humanity, their insights about mental illness or mental wellness are not necessarily meaningless for those who embrace religious beliefs. Their error was not so much in the absence of truths in their theories, but that the emphasis was upon their particular hypothesis as being *the foundation* of all mental health. Childhood experiences, environmental surroundings, self-confidence, and core beliefs all play an important role in understanding and developing a strong mind.

> *"The terrible thing about our time is precisely the ease with which theories can be put into practice. The more perfect, the more idealistic the theories, the more dreadful is their realization. We are at last beginning to rediscover what perhaps men knew better in very ancient times."*[1]
>
> —Thomas Merton

Today's mental health professionals and the general public would likely agree that the manner in which we are raised, as well as our childhood experiences, positive and negative, strongly influence who we are and how we behave as adults—a Freudian theory. Sociological studies continually support the traditional idea that parenting is the single most influential and important factor in raising children. A personal example illustrates this idea.

While I enjoy an occasional cigar, I have never had the slightest temptation to smoke cigarettes. Although my parents never approved of or used tobacco, it was not their censure, the Surgeon General's warning, or the threat of lung cancer that kept me from smoking, but a vivid childhood experience. I was raised sixth in a family of seven children, with older brothers two and five years my senior who were my first heroes. As the youngest boy, I fully admit to being gum stuck to their shoes. I

---

1. Thomas Merton, *Conjectures of a Guilty Bystander* (Garden City, NY: Doubleday, 1966), 98.

was too little and young to be of any use but always pestering to be "one of the guys."

One day during my seventh summer I refused to leave the wooded hideout where my brothers and friends were giggling with preteen excitement over the forbidden fruit of a pack of cigarettes. They refused my pestering to join in, but with a persistent whining I wore them down. They handed me one with a this'll-teach-ya smirk on their faces, and I inhaled. I can't recall precisely what happened next, as the sound of their hysterical laughter was drowned by my ceaseless coughing and watering eyes! That simple childhood experience was for me more than enough to deter even the mildest temptation to begin smoking.

Behavioralists in the tradition of Watson and Skinner have made the case for a person's environment impacting behaviors. While they took this view to its extreme, there are certainly elements of truth here. I observed the role environment plays when I worked as a youth counselor at a boot camp treatment facility for delinquent offenders. Most of the kids we worked with were fairly tough, coming from an inner-city environment. Frequently they spoke proudly of their gang affiliations, which was understandable considering that there were often no parents around to fill the vital role of family. These youth had already received some community-based counseling, and many had also been through placement in more traditional, less rigid residential treatment facilities. There were a few young men who had literally spent half their lives in various facilities, accepting the fate that they would never live outside of the criminal justice system.

On day one of the 15-week program cadets arrived with the intense mannerisms, attitudes, experiences, and personal beliefs that mirrored the rough street environment in which they lived. These characteristics were typified by anger, hostility, resentment, self-absorption, and intemperance. At the moment of their arrival, their new environment changed *dramatically*.

These kids lost their freedom by the inability to live inside the law, but their new surroundings were marked by a complete loss of personal liberties. They were told when to wake, what to wear, what to eat, how to speak, what to think, and when to sleep. As the name *boot camp* suggests, the program was designed around the military concept of breaking down toxic individualism, while building discipline and esprit de corps. The daily regimen began with physical training, was followed by school, and continued with group and individual counseling, with limited time for earned recreation. Every day was the same.

What was striking about this work was the undeniable change seen in the majority of those who completed the program. Their crusty and defiant attitude was gradually but undeniably replaced by a demeanor that closely resembled that of a soldier. By graduation most cadets were walking tall. The single most striking difference was not that these cadets would look others in the eye, but the look in their eyes. They had made it through camp and accomplished something big! The flip side of this coin is that these youth did not receive orders for a unit assignment, as soldiers do. They returned to their communities and the same environment from which they came. Unfortunately for many of these young men that meant behavioral regression and future encounters with the law.

> *"Let not a man guard his dignity,*
> *but let his dignity guard him."*[2]

—RALPH WALDO EMERSON

Carl Rogers and other humanist psychologists have helped to move psychology away from the negative, rigid view of human nature found in psychoanalysis and behavioralism. By highlighting the inherent value and goodness found in people, this school of thought elevates the level of dignity seen in humanity. People are viewed as *more* than the sum or their subconscious or mere effects of their environmental circumstances. Understood as more fully human, people can exercise their will and insight to find meaning and purpose in life.

A dramatic and sober example of this principle can be seen in the life experience and work of Austrian psychiatrist Victor Frankl (1905–1997). During World War II Frankl spent more than two and one-half years in concentration camps, and he was subject to the brutal cruelty that typified the Nazi regime. In his book *Man's Search for Meaning*[3] Frankl details these experiences, which include vicious beatings, starvation, rampant disease, physical exhaustion, and extreme mental anguish. This tragic chapter in history was made possible only because of the absolute rejection of inherent human dignity, with concentration camp prisoners being seen as animals.

Frankl's reflections about surviving this horrific experience deepened his understanding about an individual's intrinsic worth and the critical importance of self respect. Each human being is

---

2. As cited in Michael Moncur, The Quotations Page, "Ralph Waldo Emerson," 1994–2007, http://www.quotationspage.com/quote/29048.html.

3. Victor E. Frankl, *Man's Search for Meaning: An Introduction to Logotherapy* (Boston: Beacon Press, 1959).

to be understood as unique, as having extraordinary value that is a particular characteristic of humanity. By our very nature we transcend animals. We have as part of our being an internal existence that is free to choose our response to life. Once we can see and embrace our significance, we can live with dignity even when circumstances are inhumane. Frankl, along with millions of holocaust victims, experienced such savagery that can only be understood by those who suffered it. His understanding of the value and dignity of life was forged in the fires of what must have been hell on Earth. He was stripped of all material resources, subject to physical and mental torture, and left with no outward reason for existence. Yet it was in the depths of hopelessness that Frankl found not only inner freedom but a sovereignty that could not be taken from him. This liberty is found in the inherent dignity of the human person.

Victor Frankl's experience in the concentration camps helps to support the humanistic call to recognize the dignity and worth in individuals. But his life and work goes beyond that and bridges the gap to the most recent theory in psychology, the cognitive view. Cognitive psychologists emphasize the critically important role a person's outlook, or *beliefs,* play in life. As human beings with free will, our principles, attitudes, and beliefs about a situation greatly impact our emotions and behaviors. Frankl goes to the heart of this when he writes,

> But what about human liberty? Is there no spiritual freedom in regard to behavior and reaction to any given surroundings? Is that theory true which would have us believe that man is no more than a product of many conditional and environmental factors—be they of biological, psychological or sociological nature? Is man but an accidental product of these? Most important, do the prisoners' reactions to the singular world of the concentration

camp prove that man cannot escape the influences of his surrounding? Does man have no choice of action in the face of such circumstances? We can answer these questions from experiences as well as on principle. The experiences of camp life show that man does have a choice of action. There were enough examples, often of a heroic nature, which proved that apathy could be overcome, irritability suppressed. Man *can* preserve a vestige of spiritual freedom, of independence of mind, even in such terrible conditions of psychic and physical stress… everything can be taken from a man but one thing: that last of the human freedoms—to choose one's attitude in any given set of circumstances, to choose one's own way. [4]

While there are elemental truths found in each of the four main psychotherapeutic approaches, few would continue to argue that any single view captures all human behaviors. Our upbringing, living environments, instincts, and beliefs all serve to color the portrait that depicts our life. Our existence as human beings simply transcends any one-dimensional explanation, as sophisticated as that description may be.

---

4. Ibid., 86.

6

Closing the Loop

"The man who has no inner life is the slave of his surroundings."[1]

—Henri Frederic Amiel

THE COGNITIVE view in psychology, arguably the leading approach to understanding how the mind works, can serve as a link between understanding how both psyche and spirit influence mental wellness. How an individual perceives life as a whole, as well as in the momentary happenings that make up each day must influence our feelings, thoughts and actions. Our worldview, the "big pictures" we all have—beliefs about God, life, death, heaven, hell, the afterlife—will greatly influence how we understand our existence. These beliefs form principles that guide us, consciously or not, on a daily basis.

Although most mental health practitioners continue to work from the more traditional views of psychoanalysis, behavioralism, and humanism, cognitive therapists and scholars are arguably on the cutting edge when it comes to understanding the role of beliefs in mental health. During the past few decades researchers have begun to explore the relationships between faith beliefs and mental health, beginning to reestablish a dia-

1. As cited at Refdesk.com, Thought-of-the-Day Archives, September 2001, "Henri Frederic Amiel," 1995–2008, http://www.refdesk.com/sep01td.html.

logue in psychology that has been severed for the better part of a century.

For example, religion has been described as an "orienting worldview"[2] because faith often guides the development of our moral belief, which in turn guides our behaviors. Spirituality has been understood as a type of intelligence, and as it relates to cognition has been described as the "Psychology of Ultimate Concern."[3] Through spiritual practice many people develop a belief regarding their ultimate purpose in life. The goal of this vision is union with a Supreme Being. This decisive purpose motivates self-awareness and encounters with others. There is also a growing recognition that science will simply not answer many of life's questions or explain all problems. Secular scientists and materialists call for a world where we only accept those facts that can be tested, quantified, analyzed, and proven. Regardless of a person's faith belief, much of life is a mystery and will remain a mystery. We can analyze a parent's love for his or her child, postulate about life after death, and hypothesize why some people prefer beer while others enjoy wine, but we can never mechanically account for the mystery of our existence.

Many scholars break with tradition and align with the general public's endorsement of the importance and value of faith beliefs and character in life. Research and polls continually show that a high percentage of Americans believe in God. Even in much of the academic world, which has historically been hostile toward faith beliefs, there is a strong, new interest in looking at this subject from a scientific viewpoint. However, one of the

2. Gregory R. Peterson, "Religion as Orienting Worldview," *Zygon*, 36, no.1 (2001): 5.

3. Robert A. Emmons, "Is Spirituality Intelligence? Motivation, Cognition, and the Psychology of Ultimate Concern," *International Journal for the Psychology of Religion* 10, no. 1 (2000): 3.

challenges in discussing a scientific examination of faith is describing exactly what is meant by *religion* and *spirituality*.

DEFINING RELIGION AND SPIRITUALITY

Virtually all of the studies that examine the relationship between faith beliefs and physical or mental wellness discuss the similarities and differences between spirituality and religion. *Spirituality* is generally understood as the pursuit of that which is sacred in life and beyond, which gives meaning to the material, physical elements of the human condition. On the other hand, *religion* tends to refer to a person's involvement with an organized social group that is centrally concerned with spiritual matters. Both of these concepts are multidimensional. Religion consists of participation in a faith organization with established rituals intended to support a person's relationship with the Divine. Spirituality is often learned and practiced within some organized group. Spirituality is not necessarily dependent upon organized religion, nor is formal religious membership a prerequisite for spiritual practice.

Regular attendance at a church, temple, or mosque does not guarantee individuals a higher degree of belief in God than non-attendees hold. Regretfully, many individuals have manipulated noble tenets of religion in order to spread evil and engage in horrible actions. Critics of religion accurately point out that there are historical accounts of atrocities committed in the name of God. During the Middle Ages the Crusades were literally a holy war between the religions of Christianity, Judaism, and Islam. Modern time has not eliminated ongoing conflicts, including killings between Catholics and Protestants in Northern Ireland. American soldiers are currently fighting a war in the Middle East, which has been heavily influenced by ideological, religious differences. Atheists, agnostics, and other opponents of religion will often cite these and similar examples of violence committed in the name of religion as the argument against faith beliefs. This criticism highlights the need to avoid a shallow approach to faith that only examines surface attachment to a religious label. There are cases throughout history of ruthless men who intertwined warped ideologies with religious principles to satisfy corrupt goals.

Perhaps the most notorious example of such a man during the past century was Adolf Hitler. Hitler was baptized and raised in the Catholic faith, and he imbued his National Socialist German Workers' Party (NAZI) with a twisted religious identity.[4] Hitler's true beliefs and motives scorched any authentic tie to Christianity as he commanded genocide in pursuit of a pure Aryan race, engulfing all of humanity in the Second World War. His corrupt and diabolic policies eventually led to the Holocaust of six million Jews and three million Catholics.[5] The first concentration camp was built near the Bavarian town of Dachau, and it was also used as the chief concentration camp for Christian prisoners. At least 30,000 of the 200,000 prisoners confined at Dachau were killed, with thousands more dying as a result of their treatment in captivity. More than 2,700 of the captives were clergy, mostly polish priests, and others who held religious beliefs that posed a threat to Nazi tyranny.[6]

There are many today who equate religion with dark-age thinking, and some blame religious conviction as the cause of

---

4. "Pope Pius XII and the Holocaust" online pamphlet printed by A Catholic Response, Inc., Lincoln, NE, May 27, 1998, http://users.binary.net/polycarp/piusxii.html.

5. Ibid.

6. William J. O'Malley, "Appendix A: The Priests of Dachau," *Pius XII and the Holocaust*, A Reader, 1988. Printed at Catholic League for Religious and Civil Rights Web site, http://www.catholicleague.org/piusxii_and_the_holocaust/append_a.htm.

many atrocities. Their case is made anemic by the simple fact that there has been more mayhem resulting from atheist or agnostic leaders during the past century than all religious war crimes of the past two millenniums. One regime, the Khmer Rouge, murdered two million Cambodians, *25 percent of the country's population*, between 1975 and 1979.[7] Led by the atheist Saloth Sar, popularly known as Pol Pot, the Khmer Rouge ruthlessly committed genocide against Vietnamese living in Cambodia, also targeting individuals because of their religion, ethnicity, Western education, or other attributes. Inspired by a visit to Communist China, Pol Pot wanted to establish an idealized peasant agrarian society. To do so he would need to cleanse Cambodia from religion, capitalism, urban life, and all Western influences. Pol Pot evacuated all city residents by foot into slave labor camps, where many died from exhaustion, disease, torture, or execution. These tragic events were captured in the 1984 movie *The Killing Fields*. Pol Pot, like Joseph Stalin a half century before, was an atheist responsible for the massacre of millions. Still, it would be ludicrous to suggest that because these dictators were atheists, secularists have a tendency toward genocide.

Critics of religion must understand our human limitations. Just as our bodies are mortal, our intellects will never reach a point of omnipotence where we can read the minds of terrorists like Joseph Stalin, Adolf Hitler, Pol Pot, or the leaders of the 1994 Rwanda genocide. Evil, sin, disturbance, or sickness, by whatever term, has been part of human history.

---

7. At cited in United Human Rights Council, "Cambodia Genocide (Pol Pot)," Glendale, CA, http://www.united humanrights.org/Genocide/pol_pot.htm.

CAN REASON AND FAITH COEXIST?

Before reviewing scientific research studies that support faith beliefs and mental wellness, it is important to throw some water on the rhetorical flames that claim faith and reason, religion and science are not only incompatible but that they have been historically combative. There are certainly many today who take up this battle. Logic warriors make the stand that the only way to live is to trust solely in personal experience and in what has been proven true by empirical science. These individuals believe faith is nothing more than the childish fantasy of simple-minded adults. On the other side are religious extremists with recruits from every faith who place little value in science or reason, believing all truth is embodied and revealed only through their particular deity. Troops from this unit dismiss legitimate scientific discovery as the blasphemous work of souls doomed to punishment for heathen beliefs.

These hostilities are a relatively new conflict. Prior to the twentieth century faith and reason were seen as complementary in one worldview. For several hundred years one of the most dominant worldviews in Western civilization was known as the "two books" of knowledge, which refers to understanding mankind's place in the world through reading sacred Scripture and nature.[8] Belief in God had been consistent with discoveries about how creation (nature) operates. This changed in large part due to Darwin's seminal work on evolution, *On the Origin of Species,* in 1859. His proposition that humans descended from apes had the effect of making people choose sides—soulless creatures or spiritual beings with physical mortality.

In addition to Darwin's book, this division was encouraged by the publication of two popular works that intentionally

---

8. Counterbalance Foundation Web site, "Ron Numbers," Seattle: WA, http://www.pbs.org/faithandreason/transcript/num-frame.html.

painted religion as the enemy of science. The first book was titled *History of the Conflict between Religions and Science,*[9] written in 1874 by John William Draper, professor of chemistry at the University of New York. Draper's work painted religion as being at war against science. He argued that religion had historically opposed the use of science and reason, and he was especially caustic toward the Catholic Church, writing, "In the Vatican—we have only to recall the Inquisition—the hands that are now raised in appeals to the Most Merciful are crimsoned. They have been steeped in blood!"[10] The second of these influential works, *A History of the Warfare of Science with Theology in Christendom,*[11] was written in 1896 by Andrew Dickson White. White held an influential position as the first president and co-founder (along with Ezra Cornell) of Cornell University, and he devoted much of his writings and lectures to arguing that Christianity had been at war against science. He admired Draper's work and was a stalwart supporter of science, reflecting, "More and more I saw that it was the conflict between two epochs in the evolution of human thought—the theological and the scientific."[12] White was less militant than Draper, targeting doctrinal theology as opposed to more general religious beliefs. Both of these bestselling works served to popularize the perception that religion and science are diametrically opposed to one another. Margaret Wertheim, a scholar who has written and lectured extensively about the history of science and religion notes, "Although at the time there were many people—both scientists and religious

9. John W. Draper, *History of the Conflict between Religion and Science* (New York: D. Appleton, 1887).

10. Ibid., xi.

11. Andrew D. White, *A History of the Warfare of Science with Theology in Christendom* (New York: Dover, 1896), ix.

12. Ibid.

believers—who did not see a conflict between the two worlds, the warfare view became deeply entrenched in many people's minds, and it has continued to influence thinking throughout the twentieth century."[13]

Prior to this time in history there was no such "warfare" mentality. Most of the early pioneers of science were profoundly religious individuals who believed that scientific discoveries would enhance faith. Among these were Robert Grosseteste, Bishop of Oxford and prominent defender of mathematical science during the Middle Ages; Roger Bacon, the brilliant Franciscan monk who was an early proponent of the scientific method; and Nicholas of Cusa, the Roman Catholic cardinal and astronomer who defended the idea of an infinite universe. In addition to these there were the three pioneers of heliocentric cosmology (sun at the center of the universe), Nicholas Copernicus, Johannes Kepler, and Isaac Newton, who all believed that scientific discoveries would reveal God's hand in creation and nature.[14] Newton, who had an especially strong faith, believed, "There is no other way (without revelation), to know God but by the manifestations in nature."[15]

The antagonism which exists today between religion and mental health, much like religion and science, was not as prevalent before the development of psychology as a strict scientific discipline. Some of the earliest and finest care given to the mentally ill in the Western world was provided by religious groups. One of the first hospitals to serve people's mental needs was established in AD 490 by religious groups in Jerusalem. Before

13. Margaret Wertheim, contributor, "History," Counterbalance Foundation website, Seattle, WA, www.counterbalance.net/introvid/histo-body.html.

14. Ibid.

15. As cited in Gale E. Christianson, *In the Presence of the Creator: Isaac Newton and His Times* (New York: Free Press, 1984), 257.

such interventions people thought to be psychologically ill or evil were treated harshly, typically warehoused in prison-like dwellings. In the sixth century the mentally sick were cared for in church monasteries, and by the twelfth century some of the needy were even brought into Christians' homes in certain parts of Europe.

The great theologian Thomas Aquinas (1225–1274) worked to synthesize religious teaching and Aristotelian philosophy. His work was widely embraced by scientists in the middle of the fourteenth century. Aquinas emphasized the meaning of dreams and functions of the unconscious mind centuries before Freud did so.

Church-sponsored asylums were first established in Spain during the early 1400s. Near the end of the Middle Ages, religious scientists proposed that biological causes spurred many mental problems. It was the Quakers who bought moral treatment beliefs to America, and for the next hundred years, spiritual and religious principles were used in the treatment of the mentally ill.[16]

Science *can* learn from religion. Spiritual beliefs and practice, on the other hand, can benefit from the findings of science. Both can and should complement one another. More importantly, they have begun to do so.

---

16. Harold G. Koenig and David Larson, "Religion and Mental Health: Evidence for an Association," *Review of Psychiatry* 13, no. 2 (2001): 67–78.

THE THREE-LEGGED STOOL

"We must no more ask whether the soul and body are one than ask whether the wax and the figure impressed on it are one."[17]

—ARISTOTLE

The growing interest in faith and mental wellness has been outpaced by the now-established connection between mind and body in medical science. The biomedical view of illness, which confronts sickness by treating only the body, has served as the standard approach to health treatment for the past few centuries. While enormous advances have been made using this approach, especially in surgical and pharmacological applications, there has been growing recognition that even more could be done if the entire person were treated.[18] We are departing from a one-dimensional view of health toward more holistic forms of healing. This shift in treatment steps away from the biomedical view of sickness toward an integrative treatment model—one that embraces the importance of one's mind, body, and spirit as powerful contributors to wellness.

It is interesting to note that although this is a relatively modern shift in understanding health in our culture, all cultures throughout recorded history have practiced some form of mind-body healing. It was only 300 years ago, during the Enlightenment of the eighteenth century, that a rigid medical model began to separate the functions of body and mind. This mechanical view of medicine was firmly established during the early twentieth century due to the scientific ability to control several infectious diseases, such as tuberculosis, and smallpox.

---

17. As cited in Quotations of Wisdom, 2007, http://quotationsofwisdom.com/?menu_id=7&id=2083.

18. Herbert Benson, "The Three-Legged Stool," *Mind Body Medicine: A Journal of Clinical Behavioral Medicine* 1, no. 1 (1995): 1–2.

Yet prevalence of these diseases was already in decline due to enhanced sanitation, improved water quality, and better nutrition. We have reached a point in modern nations where illness and death are caused more by lifestyle choices than biologically based infectious diseases.[19]

Mind-Body Connections

Walter Cannon ignited the current medical interest featuring the impact of the mind on the body during the 1930s. Cannon (1871–1945) was a physiologist at Harvard Medical School who studied the fight-or-flight response. The fight-or-flight response describes the physical reaction of people—who will either fight or flee—when faced with an immediate threat. Cannon discovered that numerous physiological changes occur in response to what he termed the "emergency reaction." Some of these changes include increases in skeletal-muscle activity, central nervous system arousal, and sympathetic nervous system activity. He also described the associated physical changes with this reaction, including increased blood sugars and blood flow to the heart, lungs, and muscles and reduction in blood flow to the stomach area and extremities.[20]

During the 1950s physiologist Hans Selye (1907–1982) conducted research on the effects of the "fight-or-flight response" on the nervous and glandular systems. Selye, building on the work of Cannon, developed what he termed the General Adaptation Syndrome to describe the body's general response to heightened

19. Kenneth R. Pelletier, "Mind as Healer, Mind as Slayer: MindBody Medicine Comes of Age," *Advances* 18, no. 1 (2002): 4–15.

20. Gregg D. Jacobs, "The Physiology of Mind-Body Interactions: The Stress Response and the Relaxation Response," *The Journal of Alternative and Complementary Medicine* 7, supplement 1 (2001): S-83-S-92.

levels of stress.[21] General Adaptation Syndrome (GAS) depicts how the body adapts to stress through three stages. The first is the alarm reaction, where the body readies itself to battle or retreat. This is followed by the resistance phase, where the body fights the stressor, while the initial fight-or-flight response ceases. The third level is the exhaustion phase and is marked by the body's inability to acclimatize to the stressor. Selye found that during this phase the body could become ill, suffering from effects such as shrinkage of the lymph nodes, spleen, and thymus. Under extreme degrees of stress the body is susceptible to exhaustion and death.

A large number of studies exploring the impact of stress on physical health have been conducted since the early efforts of Cannon and Selye, with nearly all indicating a consistent, scientific relationship between stressful life events and poor health. Stress can lead to birth complications, heart attacks, diabetes, and a general vulnerability to poor health. This new understanding about the negative impact of stress led researchers to question what is meant by health. Is *health* limited to our physical body? Do day-to-day life events have any relevance? Can our mind influence how our bodies function? Do beliefs matter? In answer to these questions, the past two decades has seen a movement toward a biopsychosocial-spiritual approach to health and wellness, which contrasts to the traditional biomedical view and practice of medicine. As the term suggests, this approach to health considers physical, mental, social, and spiritual factors that influence physical health.

Psychiatrist George Engel (1913–1999) was among the first to challenge strict reliance upon the traditional medical model of illness, proposing a more holistic biopsychosocial approach to health and wellness. In his now classic article titled "The Need for

---

21. Ibid.

a New Medical Model: A Challenge for Biomedicine,"[22] Engel makes the case that all of medicine—not psychiatry alone—is in a crisis state due to reliance upon an antiquated worldview. He makes the important point that the biomedical view of illness has calcified into dogmatic standing. An unbendable belief that physiochemical origins account for nearly all physical and mental distress ignores social, emotional, and behavioral contributors to health and illness. Engel also highlights the anguish of the psychiatry profession in trying to keep up with the monumental advancements made by its elder brother in medicine. He writes that psychiatrists "are today so preoccupied with their own professional identity and status in relation to medicine that many are failing to appreciate that psychiatry now is the only clinical discipline within medicine concerned primarily with the study of man and the human condition."[23]

Cardiologist Dr. Herbert Benson is one of the leading researchers on mind-body interaction. During the 1970s he observed that many of his patients had high blood pressure readings during normal examinations. Hypothesizing that stress was to blame, he returned to his alma mater, Harvard Medical School, with the hopes of discovering a model for stress-induced hypertension. Using biofeedback technology he trained squirrel monkeys to either lower or raise their blood pressure through operant conditioning. His study revealed that monkeys receiving rewards had high blood pressure readings and eventually developed hypertension as a result of their own behaviors.[24]

22. George L. Engel, "The Need for a New Medical Model: A Challenge for Biomedicine," *Science* 196, no. 4286 (April 8, 1977): 129–36. Citations are to the reprinted article in *Family Systems Medicine* 10, no. 3 (1992).

23 Ibid., 327.

24. Herbert Benson, "Mind-Body Pioneer," *Psychology Today*, 34, no. 3 (May/June 2001): 56–60.

Benson was also interested in meditation, a classic Eastern mind-body technique. He conducted research monitoring the subject's heart rate, brain waves, blood pressure, metabolism, and breathing rate in two settings: first, when the individuals sat silently for 20 minutes, and second, when they engaged in 20 minutes of meditation. Benson stated that his findings were "astounding," and that "through the simple act of changing their thought patterns, the subjects experienced decreases in their metabolism, breathing rate and brain wave frequency."[25] The author labeled these changes the "relaxation response"—the opposite of the "flight-or-fight" response.

Benson suggests that the relaxation response can be activated by several meditative methods, including rhythmic prayer, qigong, progressive muscle relaxation, diaphragmatic breathing, jogging, and even knitting. He suggests that the relaxation response is an innate response to compensate for the stress response, and he highlights four elements that need to be present to enable the reaction. These include calm surroundings, disregard for daily thought, relaxed body posture, and center of attention placed on a repetitive mental stimulus, such as a sound, phrase, word, or rhythmic breathing. Benson's model has broad support, and is used to explain the healing effects of the relaxation response on a variety of health problems.

Benson's theory evaluating the effect of mind-body interventions and the relaxation response was tested on college students in 2002.[26] Researchers studied the effect of a six-week mind-body program on students' stress level. Their hypothesis was that students who received training in mind-body tech-

25. Ibid., 58.

26. Gloria R. Deckro and others, "The Evaluation of a Mind/Body Intervention to Reduce Psychological Distress and Perceived Stress in College Students," *Journal of American College Health* 50, no. 6 (2002): 281–90.

niques would experience reduced levels of psychological stress compared with those in a group without the training. The 128 students were randomly assigned to experimental and control groups. Those in the control group did not receive training during the study, while students in the experimental group attended six, weekly 90-minute group training classes. The mind-body techniques presented included a variety of relaxation response methods, as well as cognitive behavioral interventions, such as awareness of one's thoughts and their effect on emotions. Students were encouraged to use these methods regularly.

Three standardized psychological instruments gauged the mental state of the students before and after the training. The results indicated a significant improvement regarding the awareness of anxiety and the ability to deal with stress for the treatment group, compared with the control group. The authors concluded that their findings support previous studies that demonstrate stress level reductions through the use of mind-body interventions. They added that while their study has limitations, their findings confirm the effectiveness of the reaction response and cognitive behavioral interventions.

Medical Versus Holistic Health Care

We are hopefully reaching a point where we are rediscovering the mystery of the human person and maturing beyond the often compulsive desire to empirically explain every facet of life. Science has made remarkable discoveries and will continue to benefit humankind in ways now unimaginable. However, we must not give into the temptation to believe knowledge is the same as wisdom or that discovery equates with destiny. The best and brightest of all ages share common mortality, a limited time on earth. Making the case that it's now time for a biopsychosocial-spiritual view of health care with the end of life in mind Daniel Sulmasy, Ph.D., writes,

> The experiences of both patients and practitioners at the dawn of the twenty-first century is that the reductivist, scientific model is inadequate to the real needs of patients who are persons. Having cracked the genetic code has not led us to understand who human beings are, what suffering and death mean . . . . All human persons have genomes, but human persons are not reducible to their genomes.[27]

These two views—biomedical and biopsychosocial—differ greatly in feel and purpose.

There is a growing attraction and expansion toward the later, which incorporates the spiritual dimension of humanity. Key distinctions separate both perspectives. Two of the more profound differences between the models involve the view of patient health[28] and role of the professional.[29] In the biomedical model, the focal point is on treating biologically based disease symptoms in a manner detached from social, emotional, and religious influences upon health. This is in contrast to the biopsychosocial or spiritual model where a holistic approach to healing is emphasized. This paradigm supposes that physical, social, psychological, and religious dimensions influence each other.

---

27 Daniel, P. Sulmasy, "A Biopsychosocial-Spiritual Model for the Care of Patients at the End of Life," *The Gerontologist*, 42, special issue 3 (2002): 25.

28. Ibid.

29. Susan S. Johnson and Robert F. Kushner, "Mind/Body Medicine. An Introduction for the Generalist Physician and Nutritionist," *Nutritional Clinical Care* 4, no. 5 (2001): 256–64.

The role of the professional in healing also differs greatly with each perspective. In the traditional model the professional is the expert who prescribes scientific interventions to alleviate symptoms. This professional's role in the biopsychosocial or spiritual treatment view turns 180 degrees, teaming the professional with the patient to work as allies toward health. The professional recommends healing intervention, but also serves as a guide or coach to help the patient move toward wellness.

The biopsychosocial-spiritual approach to medicine, also called integrative, humanistic, or mind-body medicine, is based on research findings of psychoneuroimmunology. Psychoneuroimmunology, or PNI, has emerged as the leader of the innovative medical worldview which embraces a mind-body-spirit approach to health and wellness. According to Johnson and Kushner PNI has established that thoughts and emotions have a clear impact on our neuroendocrine and immune systems. The authors state that thinking and feelings "*directly* affect health and disease. A thought or emotion can manifest itself bodily; conversely, a bodily process can translate itself into a thought or an emotion. Thoughts and emotions can alter biology, and can do so in medically consequential ways."[30]

PNI research over the past decade has proven that nerve endings exist in the spleen, thymus, and lymph nodes, and that the nervous system produces chemical signals, drawing a response from immune cells. Other scientific research sustaining a connection between the mind and body is found in studies conducted on the placebo effect. In the placebo effect a person's symptoms show improvement through what would be considered a meaningless treatment because the patient *believes* the treatment has value. Medical researchers have typically used sugar pills in place of medicines to examine how a

---

30. Ibid., 257.

person's mind and body responds to *belief.* Roughly one-third of patients display clinical improvements from taking a placebo pill for numerous medical conditions. Placebo has been shown to be half as effective in pain management as morphine or any pain reliever.[31]

The placebo effect and researchers' willingness to study it certainly imply that there may be more to the connection between mind and body than has been medically established. By acknowledging that there may be unknown forces influencing the wellness of the body, the medical field may be able to expand its understanding of available approaches to treatment.

Holistic Models

These new treatments are already becoming a reality. For nearly two decades the interest and use of alternative medicine has greatly expanded.[32] Since 2001 the National Center for Complementary and Alternative Medicine (NCCAM), one of twenty-seven institutes and centers that comprise the National Institutes of Health (NIH) within the Department of Health and Human Services, has listed "Mind-Body Interventions" as one of the four primary categories of complementary and alternative medicine (CAM). NCCAM defines CAM as a set of diverse health care systems, procedures, and products that are not currently considered part of modern medicine. While some empirical data supports the effectiveness of certain alternative

---

31. Gregg D. Jacobs, "The Physiology of Mind-Body Interactions: The Stress Response and the Relaxation Response," *The Journal of Alternative and Complementary Medicine* 7, supplement 1 (2001): S-83-S-92.

32. Paul D. Boutin, and others, "Use and Attitudes about Alternative and Complementary Therapies among Outpatients and Physicians at a Municipal Hospital," *The Journal of Alternative and Complementary Medicine* 6, no. 4 (2000): 335–43.

treatments, for most there are questions that are yet to be addressed through sound research.³³

NCCAM describes mind-body medicine as that which employs a range of methods intended to improve the mind's ability to influence physical symptoms and bodily functions. Some methods that were considered CAM in the past, such as patient support groups and cognitive-behavioral therapy are now conventional forms of treatment. Other mind-body methods are still considered CAM, including prayer and meditation, and some artistic therapies, such as music and dance. Alternative medicine is gaining the interest of professionals and being used effectively because it honors and addresses the whole person. In contrast, much of the cynicism associated with contemporary medicine is a result of treatment plans from clinicians and physicians who continue to focus almost exclusively on the body, leaving questions related to meaning to clergy and psychologists. Modern medicine will be limited in effectiveness if it disregards the mind and body, regardless of technological advances.

Progressive muscle relaxation (PMR) was one of the earliest mind-body techniques, developed by Edmond Jacobson (1888–1983) in the 1930s. Jacobson found that muscular tension accompanies stress, and he believed that by relaxing tense muscles people would experience more peaceful thoughts and emotions. PMR involves teaching patients how to tense specific muscle groups and then progressively release the tension, working all the way through the body. As individuals master this skill they are able to relieve tension throughout the entire body, enhancing health.³⁴ More popular contemporary forms of mind-

33. National Center for Complementary and Alternative Medicine, National Institutes of Health, Department of Health and Human Services, Bethesda, MD, publication no. D347, updated February 2007, http://nccam.nih.gov/ health/whatiscam/.

34. Melissa Stoppler, "Progressive Muscle Relaxation for Stress and

body treatments include yoga, qigong (a Chinese treatment combining movement, meditation, and breathing), hypnosis, and various forms of meditation.

A newer addition to mind-body technique is biofeedback. This extensively researched method of treatment uses an electronic device to provide feedback on what is normally unconscious information to an individual. This is one of the first mind-body interventions to empirically demonstrate voluntary control over the central and autonomic nervous systems. Some specific physical features that can be altered include heart rate, hand temperature, skin response, electroencephalograms (EEGs), and blood flow.

Faith and Physical Illness

During the past two decades researchers have also been exploring the role of faith beliefs on physical health. Larry Dossey is a medical doctor and leading researcher in the field of prayer and physical health. He writes that as a young physician fresh out of medical school he saw faith as little more than myth, but that time, experience, and research changed all that. In his book *Healing Words: The Power of Prayer and the Practice of Medicine*,[35] Dossey makes a powerful, scientific case for the impact of belief on physical health. He reviewed the scientific research on prayer and health, which dates back to 1872. He reviewed over 100 methodologically sound studies and found that more than half provided evidence that prayer influenced changes in living beings.

One of the more well-known studies on prayer and physical health was conducted in 1982 and 1983 by cardiologist

---

Insomnia," ed. William C. Shiel, MedicineNet.com, May 23, 2005, http://www.medicinenet.com/script/main/art.asp?articlekey=47281.

35. Larry Dossey, *The Power of Prayer and the Practice of Medicine* (New York: HarperCollins, 2003), 86.

Randolph Byrd.[36] Byrd used a computer to assign 393 patients into two groups. The first group composed of 192 patients was prayed for by home prayer groups from various religions. A second group of 201 patients did not receive this treatment. The study design was typical of those used in clinical medical research: a random, double-blind experiment in which all participants were unaware of which group they were in. Upon completion of the ten-month study there were several notable findings. The recipients of prayer were five times less likely to need antibiotics, and three times less likely to develop pulmonary edema (a condition where the lungs fill with fluid because the heart pumps improperly). No patient in the prayed-for group received intubations (an artificial airway placed in the throat), while twelve from the control group required this procedure. Every one of these outcomes was statistically significant. "Significance" in the physical and social sciences is the seal of approval, essentially a statement that a research finding has meaning and importance.

Substantial research supports a connection between prayer and physical health, but more needs to be done. Just as the medical field has benefited from research and a more holistic approach to wellness, mental health can also benefit. In the following chapter we will explore studies that show faith beliefs are not inconsequential to wellness.

36. Randolph C Byrd, "Positive Therapeutic Effects of Intercessory Prayer in a Coronary Care Unit Population," *Southern Medical Journal* 81, no 7 (1988): 826–29.

7

Reason for Faith

*"A person will worship something, have no doubt about that.
We may think our tribute is paid in secret
in the dark recesses of our hearts, but it will out.
That which dominates our imaginations and our thoughts will
determine our lives, and our character.
Therefore, it behooves us to be careful what we worship,
for what we are worshipping we are becoming."*[1]

—RALPH WALDO EMERSON

As with medicine, the mental health field is once again beginning to open up to the possibility that reason and faith complement instead of contradict one another. As the early thinkers in psychology have shown us, most of us have beliefs of some kind that not even the blanket of neutrality can cover. By their very nature religious and spiritual beliefs are intensely personal. Every human being who has ever breathed air into his or her lungs can only experience life alone. People have the ability to articulate or complete surveys *about* their beliefs, but the experience and reality of faith will always reside within each individual's mind and soul.

---

1. As cited at Thinkexist.com Quotations, copyright 1999–2006, "Ralph Waldo Emerson," http://thinkexist.com/quotation/a_person_will_worship_something_have_no_doubt/339260.html.

However, we *can* increase our understanding of why individuals value faith and how these beliefs relate to wellness. Although the majority of psychology's key theorists held an antagonistic view of faith, there were others who had a more holistic view of human nature. Swiss Psychiatrist Carl Jung (1875–1961) had beliefs about religion and mental health that serve as one such example. While distancing himself from orthodox religions, Jung believed that a spiritual component was part of the human experience. He believed that an eternal spirit has had a continual influence throughout history in ways that are beyond our comprehension. Efforts to ascribe a certain name or exacting description to this spirit were of little value. Jung, in reflecting on his treatment of many hundreds of patients, commented that of those he has cared for at or beyond middle age, the underlying problem always involved finding a spiritual perspective in life. He suggested that his patients experienced mental distress because they were unable to grasp "that which the living religions of every age have given to their followers and none of them has been really healed who did not regain his religious outlook."[2]

SUPPORT GROUPS

The most familiar and widely used behavioral treatment which embraces spirituality as a key factor is found in the various twelve-step programs, which have evolved from Alcoholics Anonymous. Alcoholics Anonymous, popularly known as AA, was founded by alcoholics Bill Wilson and Bob Smith after their meeting in Akron, Ohio, in 1935. In 1961 Wilson wrote Carl Jung a letter of appreciation for playing a key role in the development of AA. Jung graciously responded to Wilson's letter, detailing his belief

---

2. C. G. Jung, *Modern Man in Search of a Soul* (New York: Harcourt Brace Jovanovich, 1933), 229.

that psychological distress—such as addiction—may be understood as a symptom of a person who is seeking wholeness in his or her being, which might be satisfied by spiritual awareness. Jung condenses this view by pointing out that the Latin root for alcohol is *spiritus*, which is the same as *spirituality*, and creates the maxim *spiritus contra spiritum*, meaning spirits countered by the spirit.[3]

The twelve steps are comprised of belief statements that encourage addicts to accept their powerlessness over addictive behaviors and rely on a Higher Power for help. The steps include:

1. We admitted we were powerless over alcohol—that our lives had become unmanageable.

2. Came to believe that a Power greater than ourselves could restore us to sanity.

3. Made a decision to turn our will and our lives over to the care of God as we understood Him.

4. Made a searching and fearless moral inventory of ourselves.

5. Admitted to God, to ourselves, and to another human being the exact nature of our wrongs.

6. Were entirely ready to have God remove all these defects of character.

7. Humbly asked Him to remove our shortcomings.

8. Made a list of all persons we had harmed, and became willing to make amends to them all.

9. Made direct amends to such people wherever possible, except when to do so would injure them or others.

---

3. Carl Jung, letter to William G. Wilson, Jan. 30, 1961. A copy of the letter is available online at Silkworth.net, "Dr. Carl Jung's Letter to Bill W., Jan. 30, 1961," copyright 2008 silkworth.net, http://silkworth.net/aahistory/carljung_billw013061.html.

10. Continued to take personal inventory and when we were wrong promptly admitted it.
11. Sought through prayer and meditation to improve our conscious contact with God, as we understood Him, praying only for knowledge of His will for us and the power to carry that out.
12. Having had a spiritual awakening as the result of these steps, we tried to carry this message to alcoholics, and to practice these principles in all our affairs.[4]

Positive life changes are largely the result of faith. The twelve-step programs tend to emphasize the importance of a person's individual spirituality, putting less focus on institutional religions. The nature of the twelve steps is related to the axiom "religion is for people who are afraid of going to Hell . . . spirituality is for people who've been there."

Millions of people have benefited from applications of the program. Of the approximately 3.3 million people in the United States over the age of eleven who receive professional substance abuse treatment, just under than 2 million attend self-help groups such as A.A.[5] While initially developed to help alcoholics, a seemingly endless number of branch programs have grown, providing evidence of a healing experience. A small sample of offspring programs include Adult Children of Alcoholics (ACA), Workaholics Anonymous (WA), Overeaters Anonymous (OA), Sexaholics Anonymous (SA), and Recovering Couples Anonymous (RCA).

Research supports the effectiveness of AA and similar self-help programs. A three-year longitudinal study published

---

4. Bill W. and others, *Alcoholics Anonymous: The Story of How Many Thousands of Men and Women Have Recovered from Alcoholism*, 2nd ed. (New York: Alcoholics Anonymous Publishing, Inc., 1955), 59–60.

5. Stephen Magura, "The Relationship between Substance User Treatment and 12-Step Fellowship: Current Knowledge and Research Question," *Substance Use & Misuse* 42, no. 2–3 (2007): 343–60.

in 2006 reported the effectiveness of participation in recovery groups, finding that more involvement in mutual-help activities equated with decreased likelihood of substance use, or less use during relapse.[6] The benefits were seen regardless of religious affiliation, age, sex, or psychological health.

RESEARCH RESULTS

Studies have confirmed that faith contributes to good behaviorial health, positively affecting depression, suicide, substance abuse, serious mental illness, coping for the terminally ill, and overall wellness. One research study that examined the relationship between intrinsic faith and overall psychological wellness in a sample of 210 adults was conducted in 2002 by Laurencelle, Abell, and Schwartz. In this study, intrinsic faith was defined as belief and trust in Higher Power, as opposed to mere conformity with church doctrine, and the researchers used established survey instruments to assess inherent faith and several aspects of psychological health. The questions on these surveys were used to measure a person's belief in God, their mental and emotional health, and how faith beliefs impact psychological wellness. The study results indicated that people who practice high levels of faith experience lower levels of anxiety and depressive symptoms. These individuals were also more likely to be calm and emotionally balanced and less likely to have signs of an emotionally unstable personality. The researchers conclude, "Given the results described, a clear connection between intrinsic religious faith as it was defined in this study and psychological well-being appears to exist."[7] These researchers add that their findings are in line with previous research examining faith and mental health.

6. John F. Kelly and others, "A 3-Year Study of Addiction Mutual-Help Group Participation Following Intensive Outpatient Treatment," *Alcoholism: Clinical and Experimental Research* 30 (2006): 1381–92.

7. Rhonda M. Laurencelle, Steven C. Abell, and David J. Schwartz, "The Relation between Intrinsic Religious Faith and Psychological Well-

Faith beliefs have also been shown to help those who suffer from symptoms of severe psychological distress. In 2002 Phillips, Lakin, and Pargament conducted a study to explore the role of spirituality as a relevant treatment component for individuals with serious mental illness (SMI).[8] The authors identified participants with severe mental health disorders, including schizophrenia, depression, bipolar, schizoaffective (combined symptoms of schizophrenia and either depression or bipolar), and personality disorders (overly rigid patters of thoughts and behaviors). These individuals participated in a seven-week psycho-educational intervention where facilitators talked about spiritual resources (such as praying, gathering with friends, and attending religious services), life purpose, human imperfection, forgiveness, and hope. The researchers reported that the participants found a safe place for people with SMI to discuss their spiritual needs. The researchers close their report by noting, "People with SMI are spiritual as well as psychological, social and physical beings. Their spiritual issues should not be ignored or downplayed. Instead, spirituality represents a source of strength as well as burden for people with SMI that needs to be addressed by those in the mental health field."[9]

Faith practices and youth behaviors have also been explored through research. In 2001 Hodge and Cardenas examined the relationships between spiritual and religious practice and rural youth's use of alcohol, marijuana, and other illegal drugs. Two separate survey instruments measured spirituality (internal beliefs

---

being," *The International Journal for the Psychology of Religion* 12, no. 2 (2002), 120.

8. Russell E. Phillips, Rebecca Lakin, and Kenneth I. Pargament, "Development and Implementation of a Spiritual Issues Psychoeducational Group for Those with Serious Mental Illness," *Community Mental Health Journal* 38, no. 6 (2002): 467–95.

9. Ibid., 495.

about God), and religion (participation in church activities). An additional assessment gathered data regarding substance use. The researchers found that spirituality is significantly related to lower rates of marijuana and hard drug use and those adolescents with higher levels of religious involvement were significantly less likely to use alcohol than youth with less interest in religious events.[10]

Similar research was conducted examining adolescent substance abuse and religiosity with participants from both clinical (youth receiving mental health services) and non-clinical environments. Statistics generated by this study show that 12.1 percent of adolescents who scored high on faith involvement reported using alcohol, compared to 40.2 percent of youth with few religious practices. The data for drug use was comparable. Youth with more religious involvement used drugs 5.6 percent of the time, in contrast to others who abused drugs 29.3 percent of the time. Perhaps more interesting is that the results show virtually no differences between adolescents who receive mental health treatment and those who do not. The authors note that as religious practice "increases, both groups [clinical and non-clinical] reported a decrease in alcohol abuse; conversely, as religiosity wanes, reported alcohol and drug abuse increases."[11]

Depression

The National Institute of Mental Health reports that mental disorders are the leading cause of disability in the United States, with more than one-quarter (26.2 percent) of adults being af-

---

10. David R. Hodge and Paul M. Cardenas, "Substance Use: Spirituality and Religious Participation as Protective Factors among Rural Youth," *Social Work Research* 25, no. 3 (2001):153–62.

11. L. Pullen and others, "Spiritual High vs High on Spirits: Is Religiosity Related to Adolescent Alcohol and Drug Abuse?" *Journal of Psychiatric and Mental Health Nursing* 6. (1999): 6.

fected annually. Major depression is the most prominent mental illness, being diagnosed in adults at a rate of over 6 percent in any given year.[12] The diagnosis of depression and related mental health illnesses has grown exponentially during the past few decades. This is especially true for children, with an astounding 23 percent increase in diagnoses of this problem. It is little wonder that preschoolers have emerged to become leading consumers of antidepressant medication, with 25 percent (one million children) receiving the clinical label of depression.[13] Depression has become so prevalent that it has been referred to as the "common cold" of mental illness.[14]

The problem of depression is a growing concern, especially because there is no clearly established, identifiable cause for this difficulty. The popular conception is that depression is caused by chemical imbalances in the brain. Being convinced that this condition is solely biochemical in nature, many sufferers place exclusive hope in medication, dismissing psychological, social, or spiritual realities. Yet the vast majority of research on the cause of depression acknowledges that there is no singular reason for this disorder.

For the past 30 years depression has been understood

---

12. Ronald C. Kessler, "Prevalence, Severity, and Comorbidity of 12-Month DSM-IV Disorders in the National Comorbidity Survey Replication," *General Psychiatry* archives 62, no. 6 (2005): 617–27. Online at http://archpsyc.ama-assn.org/cgi/content/full/62/6/617?maxtoshow=&HITS=10&hits=10&RESULTFORMAT=&fulltext=comorbidity&searchid=1&FIRSTINDEX=0&resourcetype=HWCIT.

13. Bob Murray, Alicia Fortinberry, "Depression Facts and Stats," Uplift Program Web site, updated January 15, 2005, http://www.upliftprogram.com/depression_stats.html#3.

14. Rich Furman and Kimberly Bender, "The Social Problem of Depression. A Multi-Theoretical Analysis," *Journal of Sociology and Social Welfare* 30, no. 3 (2003): 123–37.

primarily as a single psychiatric disorder. Researchers are now seeing this problem more as a mixture of separate symptoms that differ for each individual. The symptoms may include sleep problems, ways of thinking, mood disturbances, and loss of appetite. It is generally accepted that depression *may* be caused by one or more combinations of social, psychological, or physical events. These include

- Troubling psychosocial life events, such as loss of a job, divorce, or the death of a loved one.
- Misguided ways of thinking and acting, as in low feelings of self-worth or narcissism leading to self-absorbed behaviors.
- Hormonal imbalances in the brain, popularly understood as inadequate neurotransmitters such as serotonin.

The National Institute of Mental Health and the Centers for Disease Control acknowledge that the cause of depression is unclear, and that likely numerous factors in a person's life combine to create this problem.[15] The most popular approach to treating this disorder is medical drug therapy. Media advertisements for depressive medications are becoming common, helping to solidify the normalcy of this ailment. My own work in the field attests to medication being the standard form of treatment as well. Today a visit to a psychiatrist for depressive symptoms usually leads the patient to a prescription for psychotropic medication.

Although medication is now the typical first line of offense against depression, there are more than a few dissenters in the

15. Benjamin Goldstein and Francine Rosselli, "Etiological Paradigms of Depression: The Relationship between Perceived Causes, Empowerment, Treatment Preferences, and Stigma," *Journal of Mental Health* 12, no. 6 (2003): 551–63.

medical profession who argue that the chemically imbalanced view of this problem has been exaggerated to the benefit of an enormous pharmacological system. Dr. Nathaniel Lehrman, former Clinical Director of the Kingsboro Psychiatric Center in Brooklyn, New York, has spoken out about the reliance on drug treatment for depression. In his article, "The Drug Treatment of Depression is one of the Greatest Fallacies in the History of Medicine,"[16] Lehrman argues that depression is not a medical disease, such as influenza or cancer. Instead depression is typically a mental and physical response to stressful personal and social life events. Lehrman's view of drugs and depression were seasoned through his private practice in psychiatry, which began in 1953, well before the drug age. He experienced success treating patients after identifying the cause of their depression. Lehrman sees depression as analogous to a fever, which is also a complex physical and emotional response disrupting health. He highlights the social acceptance of drug treatment, recalling Ann Landers's report on the effectiveness of National Depression Screening Day in 1998: 85,000 people were screened, and more than 70 percent were referred for complete evaluation.

The assertions made by Dr. Lehrman are serious and would likely evoke a strong response by patients who have benefited from drug treatments. However, there is little doubt that medication has taken the lead position in the race for behavioral wellness, even though the majority of scientific evidence points to aggregate causes—social stressors, hormonal imbalances, thinking errors, physical health and fitness, belief systems—as opposed to one event affecting an individual. In a 2007 book titled *The Loss of Sadness: How Psychiatry Transformed Normal*

---

16. Nathaniel D. Lehrman, "Dead Wrong: The Drug Treatment Of Depression Is One Of The Greatest Fallacies In The History Of Medicine," Depression is a Choice Web site, August 15, 2002, www.depressionisachoice.com/essays/dead_wrong.htm.

Sorrow into Depressive Disorder, Allan Horwitz and Jerome Wakefield detail how sorrow has been converted into a medical condition. The authors point out several concerning trends stemming from medicating those with ordinary sadness: the increasing consumption of anti-depressants, a distorted view of mental wellness that overlooks passing psycho-social stressors, and the push to diagnose and treat people at younger ages. The authors sum up their view, writing, "Sadness is an inherent part of the human condition, not a mental disorder. Thus to confront psychiatry's invalid definition of depressive disorder is also to consider a painful but important part of our humanity that we have tended to shunt aside in the modern medicalization of human problems."[17] The enculturation of depression understood solely as a chemical imbalance continues to have stifling effects in treatment for this problem.

Many of the clients I've worked with have developed an emotionally defensive attachment to drug therapy. By this I mean that numerous clients would scoff at the suggestion of any treatment for their illness other than drugs. One example from my work was a single mother of two who suffered from depression. There were several blatantly obvious stressors in her life. Her second marriage was new, both children were having academic and behavioral school problems, and she struggled with severe obesity. She had been prescribed medications by a psychiatrist for several years before I began to work with her. After some weeks of therapy I began introducing basic lifestyle changes. Some of these included activities, such as planning a "family night" where she could develop tighter bonds with her children. We discussed the possibility of light exercise, such as walking, to improve both her physical health and to aid with her

---

17. Allan Horwitz and Jerome Wakefield, *The Loss of Sadness: How Psychiatry Transformed Normal Sorrow into Depressive Disorder* (New York: Oxford University Press, Inc., 2007), 225.

distressful moods. In a somewhat casual yet dramatic manner she picked up her pill container and told me that all she needed was "in this little bottle," even though there had been no apparent improvement in her condition after years of drug therapy.

Psychotropic medications may be helpful for many individuals. However, scientific research has not established what has become the popular belief—that depression is *predominantly* caused by chemical imbalance, and that drugs work for most people with depression most of the time. Ironically, research has found evidence that *beliefs* about drug effectiveness are almost as powerful as the drugs themselves.

In a 2002 report titled "The Emperor's New Drugs: Analysis of Antidepressant Medication Data Submitted to the U.S. Food and Drug Administration," researchers examined the effectiveness of the six most commonly prescribed antidepressants used between 1987 and 1999, citing previous studies showing that 75 percent of medication for depression is reproduced by placebo. The six medications included Prozac, Paxil, Zoloft, Effexor, Serzone, and Celexa. In this study participants were blindly assigned to either an experimental group that received medication, or to a control group that received the sugar pill. The findings are striking. Approximately *80 percent* of the effects attributed to the medications were reproduced in the placebo control groups. While both medication and placebo were helpful in treating symptoms of depression, the data showed that drugs were only slightly more effective than sugar pills. What participants believed about medication and depression seemed to have a strong impact on their symptoms. Commenting on both their findings and the difficulty of accounting for placebo effect, the authors state, "Although our data suggest that the effect of antidepressant drugs are very small and of questionable clinical significance, the conclusion rests on the assumption that drug effects and placebo effect are additive."[18] The researchers use *additive* to mean looking at the results from both drugs *and* placebo to determine their overall effectiveness. This implies that participants *believed* their medication would relieve depressive symptoms because of its medicinal properties, when for many it was mere sugar.

Similar research was conducted in 2008 to examine the effectiveness of new generation antidepressants compared to placebo by analyzing data submitted to the United States Food and Drug Administration for the licensing of these drugs. The researchers found no significant difference between the two for patients who experienced moderate or severe depression. While these medications did produce a clinical significance for those at the very upper end of most severely depressed, this was due to a decreased response to placebo, as opposed to an increased response to the antidepressants.[19]

The perceptions and beliefs we hold are a critical factor in how we experience and live our lives. While this is true of all cultures, it may be especially relevant in our market-driven consumer society. Everything from the choice of food we eat to the clothes we wear is heavily influenced by the power of media advertisement. Medications are no exception. Television commercials and print publications promoting various brands of "happy pills" are targeted to sell by creating demand for such products. While there certainly may be legitimate value in psy-

18. Irving Kirsch and others, "The Emperor's New Drugs: An Analysis of Antidepressant Medication Data Submitted to the U.S. Food and Drug Administration," *Prevention & Treatment* 5, article 23 (2002): 1–11.

19. Irving Kirsch and others, "Initial Severity and Antidepressant Benefits: A Meta-Analysis of Data Submitted to the Food and Drug Administration," *Public Library of Science Medicine* 5, no. 2, (February 2008). Online at http://medicine.plosjournals.org/perlserv/?request=get-document&doi=10.1371/journal.pmed.0050045.

chotropic medications, it is difficult to dismiss the role advertising plays in promoting drugs as a quick fix for distress.

A 2004 report published in the *Journal of American College Health* supports this notion. Researchers in this study explored the effect that drug company advertisements have on patients' perceptions of depression and need to use antidepressant medications to treat their symptoms. The authors surveyed forty-four college students between the ages of eighteen and twenty-one and used questionnaires to collect demographic information and assess the participant's history of depression, rating symptoms as minimal, mild, moderate, or severe. The survey also evaluated participants' opinions about depression as a disorder and how it can be treated.[20]

Prior to administering the surveys the researchers randomly assigned the young adults to one of two groups: advertisement or scientific. Those in the advertisement group were provided with the publications that the drug companies used to promote their products. In general these ads implied that antidepressant use is growing due to increasing knowledge regarding the effectiveness of drug treatment. The ads also suggested that depression is widespread throughout society and that this pandemic is undertreated. Lastly, possible side-effects from taking antidepressants were provided, depicted as being rare and of little significance.

Those assigned to the scientific group were provided with more balanced and accurate information regarding both beneficial and potential harmful effects of such medications. They were given neutral information on the growing recognition of depression, enhanced treatments, and the possibility of overdiagnosis. After reading the information about depression from either an advertisement or scientific perspective, both

20. Frankenberger and others, "Effects of Information on College Students' Perceptions of Antidepressant Medication," *Journal of American College Health* 53, no. 1 (2004): 35–40.

groups completed the surveys assessing their own depression and perceptions of treatment.

The researchers found that female college students were more apt to rate their depressive symptoms as mild or moderate after reading pharmacological advertisements. More specifically, 40 percent of the females who had been exposed to drug ads rated themselves as mild, moderate, or severely depressed compared to one woman (6 percent) who had read the scientific information. The authors also found that the women in the advertisement group were much more likely to think that antidepressants were necessary to treat depression, and were more willing to suggest drug treatment to others more frequently than the women from the scientific group.

The researchers note that females generally experience depression at a higher rate than males, most college students undergo stress due to the many demands of college life, and students should "not be diagnosed with depression but should be presented with methods to reduce or cope with stress."[21] They add that college students should be educated in more holistic ways to cope with the normal pressures associated with school, including simple lifestyle changes such as a taking fewer classes, balancing work with recreation, or attending programs that target physical exercise, study skills, and sleep patterns. The researchers note that such "environmental modifications are likely to ameliorate the stressors commonly associated with college life and should be employed before more intrusive interventions such as medication are initiated." The authors suggest that pharmacological companies "should be required to provide balanced information on their Web pages and other forms of advertisement that include both the therapeutic and common

---

21. Ibid., 39.

and uncommon side effects of antidepressant medication."[22] This is good counsel in light of additional research that shows drugs have become the most accepted way to treat depression, in spite of several other interventions shown to be safer and either as helpful as or more so than antidepressant use.[23]

The National Institute of Mental Health funded a study to shed light on the commercialization of antidepressant use. The results were published in the *Journal of the American Medical Association* in 2005. In this study actors in an experimental group pretended to have either symptoms of depression or adjustment disorder and made appointments with physicians in California and New York to purposely ask for antidepressant medications. (Adjustment disorder is a disproportionate response to a negative life stressor, such as a loss of job or being involved in a car accident.) The players in the experimental group would either ask for a specific antidepressant by brand name or simply mention that they had seen commercials representing the effectiveness of drug use for depression. A second group of actors made similar appointments and claimed to be depressed or showed symptoms of adjustment disorder but did not request medication. Those who asked for drugs were significantly more likely to receive them than those who did not request a prescription. Specifically, the actors who showed symptoms of major depression and requested brand-name medication received them 53 percent of the time, and those who made a general request 76 percent of the time, compared to the actors who made no requests and received medication 31 percent of the time. Actors in the adjustment group who requested brand-name medication received it 55 percent of the

22. Ibid.

23 David O. Antonuccio, William G. Danton, Garland Y. DeNelsky, "Psychotherapy Versus Medication for Depression: Challenging the Conventional Wisdom With Data," *Professional Psychology: Research and Practice* 26, no. 6 (December 1995): 574–85.

time, while those making a general request received it 39 percent of the time. Those making no request were given a prescription only 10 percent of the time. The researchers concluded that direct marketing by pharmaceutical companies has a profound impact on drug prescription and consumption.[24]

SELF AND OTHER FOCUS

Researchers have begun to reexamine the way we understand depression in an attempt to alleviate suffering and help people experience better health and wellness. A 2004 study conducted by Lavender and Watkins examined the importance of "rumination," or self-focus, as a contributor to hopelessness about the future, which is considered a key feature of depression. Rumination is the tendency to think and talk about depressed feelings in an excessive manner.

The researchers surveyed two groups. The experimental group was made up of clinically depressed individuals, while the control group was comprised of non-depressed individuals with no history of depression. The questionnaire targeted measures to test whether focusing on oneself and his or her depression would influence a person's ability to look toward the future in a more hopeful, positive manner. Some of the questions to measure rumination included "Think about how happy or sad you feel," "Think about why you feel the way you do," and "Think about the possible consequences of the way you feel."

---

24. R. L. Kravitz and others, "Influence of Patients' Request for Direct Consumer Advertised Antidepressants: A Randomized Controlled Trial," *Journal of the American Medical Association* 293, no. 16 (2005): 1995–2002. Cited from online press release at National Institute of Mental Health, "Actor-Patients' Requests for Medication Boost Prescribing for Depression," April 27, 2005, http://www.nimh.nih.gov/science-news/2005/actor-patients-requests-for-medications-boost-prescribing-for-depression.shtml.

The effect of rumination was measured against "distraction," or thinking beyond self by focusing on external thoughts and ideas. Examples of these measures included "Think about a ship crossing the ocean," or "Think about the Mona Lisa," or some similar pleasant thought not about oneself. The researchers found that rumination tended to increase a person's sense of being depressed for persons who are already clinically depressed, but not for non-depressed individuals. The implications from this study are insightful. Symptoms of depression are not problems that should be ignored or taken lightly because they can lead to very serious emotional and physical problems. However, placing continual focus on negative thoughts and feelings will not relieve those emotions, and will likely make the depressive symptoms more severe.[25] The problems created by hopelessness are exacerbated in a culture that places ever-increasing emphasis upon material consumption as a way to satisfy the self.

Much of the current research explores those thoughts and behaviors that may be inversely related to symptoms of depression. An example of this is a 2001 longitudinal study that explored the importance of mattering to others as a protective element against depression. The concept of mattering is simply the belief that others are interested and concerned for us. The idea of being valued by others helps individuals deal with life's challenges. The authors of this study state that mattering shares common ground with purpose in life, and they review previous research arguing that purpose in life "is not a contributor to but rather a defining element of psychological well-being."[26]

25. Ana Lavender and Edward Watkins, "Rumination and Future Thinking in Depression," *The British Journal of Clinical Psychology* 43, part 2 (2004): 130.

26. John Taylor and others, "A Longitudinal Study of the Role of Significance of Mattering to Others for Depressive Symptoms, *Journal of Health and Social Behavior* 42, no. 3 (2001): 311.

The researchers examined responses from 1,300 interviews with adults age 18 to 55. The interviews contained demographic information and participant responses to a series of questions regarding depression, social support, and personal resources. To assess "mattering" participants were questioned, "How important are you to others," "How much do others pay attention to you," "How much would you be missed if you went away," and "How much do others depend upon you." The authors found that mattering does serve as a protective factor against depression for women, but not necessarily for men. This is partially explained by gender role difference, as women scored much higher on these mattering responses than men.

Faith and Depression

> *"Depression is the impression left by fear."*[27]
> —A. J. Russell

For more than a decade there has been a growing interest in the role of faith beliefs as a protective element against the difficult problem of depression. The "newfound" recognition of spirituality and religion as an important protective counter against depression should come as no surprise to anyone, especially considering that faith beliefs are inspired by ideals that facilitate happiness. A 2004 General Social Survey asked a sample of Americans about happiness and religion, with response options of "very happy, pretty happy, or not too happy." Those who believed in God were more than twice as likely to describe themselves as "very happy" (43 percent to 21 percent), and non-believers were almost three times as likely to say they were "not

---

27. A. J. Russell, ed., *God Calling: By Two Listeners* (Westwood, NJ: Barbour and Company, Inc., 1985), 243.

too happy" (21 percent to 8 percent). People of faith were also more likely to be optimistic about the future compared to secularists (34 percent to 24 percent).[28]

Faith beliefs, by their very nature, tend to offer people deep meaning and perspective about life's events, whether or not the experience is pleasant or distressful. In a 1996 article titled "Spiritual Wellness and Depression," Charlene Westgate reviewed the academic literature from the medical and counseling fields and labeled four dimensions of spiritual health that are relevant in the treatment and prevention of depression. These include 1) purpose in life; 2) intrinsic values; 3) transcendence; and 4) community support.[29]

Purpose in life has been recognized in the writings of existential psychologists such as Victor Frankl and Carl Jung, and it refers to the belief that we serve some worthy purpose in life beyond our own self. This way of thinking contrasts with some common depressive symptoms, such as lacking goals or seeing no reason for life. Intrinsic values equate with a person's core beliefs that guide his or her actions. These centering values help to form an individual's conscience, guide behavior, and protect against desires that may ultimately be psychologically unhealthy. Transcendence relates to having a relationship with a Higher Power. Belief in God gives people a larger purpose than themselves and a sense of joy and wonder when pondering all of creation. Westgate adds that this belief may counter the egocentric tendency of some depressed individuals, which may be intensified by our vain culture. The final dimension, community

28. Arthur C. Brooks, "The Ennui of Saint Theresa: On average, religious people are much happier than nonreligious ones," *Wall Street Journal*, September 30, 2007. Available online at http://www.opinionjournal.com/extra/?id=110010672.

29. Charlene E. Westgate, "Spiritual Wellness and Depression," *Journal of Counseling and Development* 75, (1996): 34.

support, refers to the shared symbols and support usually found in faith communities. This sense of unity may be especially relevant to depressed individuals, who typically report a lack of attachment to others, leading to further withdrawal and isolation. Westgate concludes her review of the literature by noting that "a powerful argument has been made for an association between spiritual void and depression. The depressed person describes symptoms that typically include meaninglessness, emptiness, and hopelessness, as well as a sense of alienation from values and a narcissistic focus" and it would be irrational to "ignore the spiritual dimension as the realm of inspiration, creativity, intuition, and values."[30]

A 2003 study carried out by Pearce, Little, and Perez examined the relationship between religious beliefs and depressive symptoms among adolescents. Three research questions were asked in this study. The first was to see if the three measures of religiosity typically used when studying adults—church attendance, private practices such as prayer, and self-ranking—would also suggest lower depressive symptoms in adolescents. (Self-ranking refers to the subjective importance of religion in a person's life.) The second research question asked whether parishioner support was related to depression, while the final question looked at the relationship between sex and ethnicity on religion and depression. The researchers collected data from 744 youths in grades seven, eight, and nine from a demographically diverse community in New England and found that several markers of religious involvement—such as attending faith services, self-ranking, and having positive religious experiences—were associated with lower rates of depression. The first two research questions were supported. The same three measures of religion normally used for adults were related to lower symptoms of depression in youth

30. Ibid.

as well. As suspected, perceived congregational support was shown to be a stronger buffer against depression than frequency of faith activities, while youth who had negative interpersonal experiences reported higher rates of depressive symptoms. There were no differences in measures of religiosity by sex or ethnicity, which is surprising since females and African Americans have historically reported higher numbers of those with faith beliefs than males and European Americans.[31]

A similar study was conducted in 2000 exploring faith and depression among young adults. The goal of the research project was to explore how depression and anxiety were tempered by spirituality. The assumption was that faith beliefs help to lessen the effect of stressful life events, which often produce anxiety and depression. The researchers surveyed 303 college students, assessing levels of spirituality, depression, anxiety and life stressors—such as marriage, broken relationships, death of loved ones, and academic difficulties. The study results affirmed that spirituality alleviates the tension that disruptive life events create. The authors added that this effect was more potent for depression than anxiety. [32]

Faith beliefs have also been shown to counter depression among the elderly. Researchers conducted a pilot study in 2002 to examine the effectiveness of a spiritually centered program for easing minor depression and anxiety among older adults.[33]

31. Michelle J. Pearce, Todd D. Little, and John E. Perez, "Religiousness and Depressive Symptoms among Adolescents," *Journal of Clinical Child and Adolescent Psychology* 32, no. 2 (2003): 267–76.

32. Scott J. Young, Craig S. Cashwell, and Julia Shcherbakova, "The Moderating Relationship of Spirituality on Negative Life Events and Psychological Adjustment," *Counseling and Values* 45, no. 1 (2000): 49–58.

33. Doris Rajagopal and others, "The Effectiveness of a Spiritually-Based Intervention to Alleviate Subsyndromal Anxiety and Minor

Twenty-two elderly individuals who had been diagnosed with minor depression agreed to participate in the 10-week experiment. All participants completed assessments to gauge their mental status and reasoning, degree of stress or support from others, levels of depression and anxiety, and spiritual or religious beliefs. Each person was placed in either an individual or group cohort. Eight participants were in the individual cohort, while fourteen participants were in the group cohort. The spiritual workout presented to all is known as the Prayer Wheel. The Prayer Wheel provides a structured way of connecting to the Divine and is made up of eight types of prayers, each lasting roughly five minutes. These eight categories of spiritual practices align with traditional religious prayers, such as counting your blessings, giving praise, requesting guidance and protection, asking and offering forgiveness, and placing trust in a Higher Power.

The researchers found a significant lessening of anxiety for those who prayed individually, but not for those praying within the group. The findings were reversed for depression. Those in the group experienced a decrease in depression, but individual participants did not. However, six-week follow-up data found that those who used the Prayer Wheel after completion of the formal intervention period experienced lower scores for depression, while the participants who ceased using these spiritual exercises had an increase in depression levels. While acknowledging the small sample, the authors suggest that spiritual and religious interventions are promising program models to help lessen symptoms of anxiety and depression in older adults.

A more robust study was conducted in 2004 and published in the *International Journal of Geriatric Psychiatry*. The study examined religious attendance and depression in a sample of

---

Depression among Older Adults," *Journal of Religion and Health* 41, no. 2 (2002): 153–67.

863 individuals between ages 65 and 74. Researchers found that persons who had not participated in religious services during the past half year were 2.7 times more likely to experience depression than the elderly who had taken part in faith practices. These statistics were generated after controlling for demographic variables, including income, marriage, education, employment status, gender, and health status. The researchers concluded that being involved in religious practices serves to protect the elderly from depression.[34]

Less attention has been directed toward young children and families, but the few studies that have been conducted on the relationship between religious involvement and psychological health show that faith practice by parents is related to improved home environment and child well-being, including health, social skills, and behavior. They also show that a mother's religiosity serves as a defensive shield against depressive symptoms in her children.[35]

Other Mental Illnesses

These research studies represent just a small sample of the mounting evidence that supports a positive relationship between religion and not only depression, but psychological wellness. Although most of the key psychologists for the past century proclaimed that faith beliefs were a sign of mental illness, ironically their "scientific" opinions were not based on empirical research,

---

34. Cheng-Yi Hahn and others, "Religious Attendance and Depressive Symptoms among Community Dwelling Elderly in Taiwan," *International Journal of Geriatric Psychiatry* 19 (2004): 1148–54.

35. Michele A. Schottenbauer, Stephanie M. Spernak, and Ingrid Hellstrom, "Relationship between Family Religious Behaviors and Child Well-Being among Third-Grade Children," *Mental Health, Religion and Culture* 10, no. 2 (2007): 191–98.

but on their personal reflections. Scientific data and research findings now tell a different story.

Some of the most definitive works on this topic have been conducted by Harold Koenig, M.D., professor of psychiatry and behavioral sciences at Duke University Medical Center. In his book *Faith & Mental Health: Religious Resources for Healing,* Koenig reviews a host of scientific research articles on religion and a wide range of psychiatric disorders. His review of the empirical research is thorough and timely, relying on many studies being published after the year 2000. His conclusion is simple: contemporary research now supports the idea that faith beliefs serve as a protection against anxiety, depression, and suicide. Religious involvement also helps to lessen antisocial behaviors such as crime and delinquency and serves as a shield against the problems of substance abuse for both adults and teens. Koenig summaries his findings by stating,

> Religious beliefs and practices are inversely associated with anxiety and depression in the majority of cross-sectional studies, usually predict less depression and faster recovery from depression in prospective studies, and, when examined in randomized clinical trials, religious interventions cause a faster reduction in clinical symptoms than secular therapies alone or no treatment. This is also true, in general, for negative character personality traits, antisocial activities that involve crime or delinquency, and use of drugs or alcohol. Thus, while not all studies report mental health benefits for religion, the vast majority of both qualitative and quantitative studies do. As a result, it is no longer possible to argue that religious involvement is usually neurotic, harmful, or incompatible with mental health, as once claimed.[36]

36. Harold G. Koenig, *Faith and Mental Health: Religious Resources for*

We are now beginning to rediscover what our ancestors have passed down and the great religions of the world have taught for centuries: what we believe affects how we live. Traditional mental health research has focused on why people are unhealthy. Studies of what enables individuals to live joyful, fulfilling lives has been absent until recently.

Healing (Philadelphia, PA.: Templeton Foundation Press, 2005), 112.

8

Character

"That which is oldest is most young and new. There is nothing so ancient and so dead as human novelty. The 'latest' is always stillborn. It never even manages to arrive. What is really new is what was there all the time."[1]

—Thomas Merton

PSYCHOLOGY HAS come full circle during the past century. This field of science has evolved from the view that faith beliefs damage an individual's mental health to empirically showing that religious and spiritual practices are beneficial to overall wellness. While the research findings described in this book and elsewhere attest to this certainty, faith beliefs will continue to be *faith beliefs*. Even though religious practices such as prayer, meditation, yoga, and qigong have been shown to improve health, all are based on an individual's belief and internal experience. They are not externally applied to improve a person's well-being, as is the case with medical procedures, such as casting fractured limbs, receiving anesthesia, or undergoing surgery.

Faith, by its very nature, transcends concrete evidence. By definition, faith means trusting in something or someone, as opposed to sterile knowledge about a fact. Webster's dictionary defines faith as "confidence or trust in a person or thing" and as

---

1. Thomas Merton, *New Seeds of Contemplation* (Norfolk, CT: New Directions, 1961), 107. Emphasis in original.

a "belief that is not based on proof."[2] Scientific research has been able to show the fruits of faith, but the revitalizing force that flows through the physical and mental branches remains hidden.

There is more than a little irony (if not humor) in the intense struggle that often exists between faith and science in general and religiosity and mental health in particular. Those who dismiss the relevance of beliefs when considering the human condition overlook the saturation of faith in every person's walk through life. Even with religious beliefs out of the equation, all of life involves faith. We don't even hope, but we assume we will have a tomorrow. We rarely give a second thought that our vehicle will start when we turn the key—even if we have no idea how an ignition system works. We embrace what CNN reports from around the world without observing the news firsthand. We believe our school history books, accepting the integrity of authors whom we have never met who write about events they have not witnessed. We place trust in our parents, wives, husbands, children, and friends, and we would never consider requiring they first complete a personality test to assure their mental competence.

Faith, in its many forms, saturates the human experience. Hopefully contemporary findings from research studies on religiosity and wellness will empower people of faith to once again integrate inspiring personal beliefs into mental wellness. At the same time it is certainly not the role of science to proselytize, pushing religious doctrine onto others. Nor is it appropriate for scientists to attack the spiritual strivings found in humanity, simply because this dimension defies quantification. *Research, findings,* and *logic* are not apt to sway an individual's deeply held personal conviction about what he or she understands God or a

2. *Webster's American College Dictionary*, special edition (NY: Random House, 1998), 288.

Supreme Being to be, or not to be. As the medieval theologian Thomas Aquinas noted, "To one who has faith, no explanation is necessary. To one without faith, no explanation is possible."[3]

CHARACTER AS PART OF LIFE

While faith may be seen as the intrinsic, core beliefs of an individual, character can be understood as the outward expression of those beliefs in the world in which we live. Faith is internal, character is external. Webster defines character as "the aggregate of features and traits that form the individual nature of a person" and as "qualities of honesty, fortitude, integrity, etc."[4]

Character, like faith, has been central to forming the values of virtually all cultures throughout recorded history. Societal laws and informal mores have grown from those behaviors deemed to be acceptable or unacceptable. Murder, rape, theft, and dishonesty are obvious examples of undesirable acts and qualities condemned by societies. Character traits, which are difficult to divorce from morality, have been historically dismissed as irrelevant to psychology and good mental health.

Because science has largely bypassed this critically important part of human existence does not make a person's moral fiber any less vital to wellness. While concepts such as character and integrity have been largely out of vogue in the mental health field until recently, these ideals continue to flourish in essentially all areas of human endeavor. From the serious professions of politics, to business and education, to the recreational pursuits of sports, as well as the common experiences of everyday life, character is commonly regarded as vital to living well.

---

3. As cited at Thinkexist.com Quotations, copyright 1999–2006, "St. Thomas Aquinas," http://en.thinkexist.com/quotes/St._Thomas_Aquinas/.

4. Ibid., 134.

"I have a dream that my four little children will one day live in a nation where they will not be judged by the color of their skin but by the content of their character."[5]

—MARTIN LUTHER KING, JR.

Politics

A democratic society such as ours relies on the integrity of the men and women we place in elected office. Even the daily chiding that politicians commonly receive from late-night comedians for not keeping their word once elected speaks to the high value given integrity. The yardstick by which most Americans measure a candidate's fitness for office is his or her strength of character. A 2008 Associated Press poll found that the majority of Americans, 55 percent, are most concerned with the character of a presidential nominee when deciding who to vote for, compared with 33 percent who place higher importance on the candidate's stand on specific issues.[6] Will people say what they believe, anchor their convictions in principles beyond opinion, and live those ideals, or will they exchange their integrity for political gain?

The political history of our nation is replete with examples of character, both positive and negative. The highest office in the land, president of the United States, presents a clear example of the premium placed on moral courage. All who have held that

---

5. Martin Luther King, Jr., "I Have a Dream," speech delivered at the Lincoln Memorial, August 28, 1963. Audio and written version available online at the University of Minnesota Extension Web site, http://www.extension.umn.edu/units/diversity/mlk.html.

6. Ron Fournier and Trevor Tompson, "Poll: Character Trumps Policy for Voters," The Associated Press, printed by *The Washington Post*, March 11, 2007, http://www.washingtonpost.com/wp-dyn/content/article/2007/03/11/AR2007031100121.html.

position—across political party lines—have left a legacy fashioned either by their strength or weakness of character. All former presidents have spoken about the critical importance of moral fiber in life, even though their human frailties were at times publicly exposed. Their words demonstrate this.

> *"Adversity brings out the best in a man and in a country."*[7]
>
> —JOHN F. KENNEDY

> *"Along with patriotism—understanding, comprehension, determination are the qualities we now need. Without them, we cannot win. With them, we cannot fail."*[8]
>
> —DWIGHT D. EISENHOWER

> *"If you will think about what you ought to do for other people, your character will take care of itself. Character is a by-product, and any man who devotes himself to its cultivation in his own case will become a selfish pig."*[9]
>
> —WOODROW WILSON

7. John F. Kennedy, speech as senator, Bangor, ME, September 2, 1960. John T. Woolley and Gerhard Peters, The American Presidency Project, [online], Santa Barbara, CA, University of California (hosted), Gerhard Peters (database). Available online, document archive, http://www.presidency.ucsb.edu/ws/index.php?pid=25911&st=adversity&st1=.

8. Dwight D. Eisenhower, Address at the Dinner of the American Newspaper Publishers Association, New York, April 22, 1954. John T. Woolley and Gerhard Peters, The American Presidency Project, [online], Santa Barbara, CA, University of California (hosted), Gerhard Peters (database). Available online, document archive, http://www.presidency.ucsb.edu/ws/index.php?pid=10217&st=the+qualities&st1=.

9. Woodrow Wilson, Address at the Young Men's Christian

*"Courage and perseverance have a magical talisman, before which
difficulties disappear
and obstacles vanish into air."*[10]

—JOHN QUINCY ADAMS

*"I ask that all Americans demonstrate in their personal and public lives
... the high ethical standards that are essential to good character and
to the continued success of our Nation."*[11]

—BILL CLINTON

*"Our progress and prosperity at home, our standing and influence
abroad, could never have been secured unless they rested on a solid
foundation of demonstrated integrity, high character,
and abiding faith."*[12]

—CALVIN COOLIDGE

Association's Celebration, Pittsburgh: "The Power of Christian Young Men," October 24, 1914. John T. Woolley and Gerhard Peters, The American Presidency Project, [online], Santa Barbara, CA, University of California (hosted), Gerhard Peters (database). Available online, document archive, http://www.presidency.ucsb.edu/ws/index.php?pid=65385&st=character+will+take+care&st1=.

10. As cited in Michael Moncur, The Quotations Page, "John Quincy Adams," 1994-2007, http://www.quotationspage.com/quote/1593.html.

11. William J. Clinton, Presidential Proclamation 7043—National Character Counts Week, October 17, 1997. John T. Woolley and Gerhard Peters, The American Presidency Project, [online], Santa Barbara, CA, University of California (hosted), Gerhard Peters (database). Available online, document archive, http://www.presidency.ucsb.edu/ws/index.php?pid=53433&st=high+ethical&st1=.

12. Calvin Coolidge, Address Dedicating the Fredericksburg and Spotsylvania Country Battle Fields Memorial, Fredericksburg, VA, October 19, 1928. John T. Woolley and Gerhard Peters, The American Presidency Project, [online], Santa Barbara, CA, University of California (hosted), Gerhard Peters (database). Available online, document archive, http://www.presidency.ucsb.edu/ws/index.php?pid=464&st=character&st1=.

> *"We must adjust to changing times and still hold to unchanging principles."*[13]
>
> —JIMMY CARTER

> *"With all the power that a President has, the most important thing to bear in mind is this: You must not give power to a man unless, above everything else, he has character. Character is the most important qualification the President of the United States can have."*[14]
>
> —RICHARD M. NIXON

> *"In the long run the one vital factor in the permanent prosperity of the country is the high individual character of the average American worker, the average American citizen, no matter whether his work be mental or manual, whether he be farmer or wage earner, business man or professional man."*[15]
>
> —TEDDY ROOSEVELT

> *"Honesty is the first chapter in the book of wisdom."*[16]
>
> —THOMAS JEFFERSON

13. Jimmy Carter, Inaugural Address, January 20, 1977. John T. Woolley and Gerhard Peters, The American Presidency Project, [online], Santa Barbara, CA, University of California (hosted), Gerhard Peters (database). Available online, document archive, http://www.presidency.ucsb.edu/ws/index.php?pid=6575&st=changing+times&st1=.

14. Television advertisement for Barry Goldwater's presidential campaign, 1964, as cited on Public Broadcasting Service, "Character Above All: Quotes," 1995–2008, http://www.pbs.org/newshour/character/quotes/.

15. Theodore Roosevelt, Fifth Annual Message to the Senate and House of Representatives, December 5, 1905. John T. Woolley and Gerhard Peters, The American Presidency Project, [online], Santa Barbara, CA, University of California (hosted), Gerhard Peters (database). Available online, document archive, http://www.presidency.ucsb.edu/ws/index.php?pid=29546&st=professional+man&st1=.

16. As cited in Trevor Hunt, ed., *Words from Our Presidents: Quips and Quotes from George Washington to George W. Bush* (NY: Gramercy Books,

"Human happiness and moral duty are inseparably connected."[17]
— GEORGE WASHINGTON

How do these words and examples of our presidents relate to mental health? They serve to highlight the importance of ideals and beliefs as guiding forces that shape our attitude about life. Since we human beings are social creatures, our mindset impacts the society in which we live. The ideas about character put forth by these men also point to how the human spirit can rise above the limitations imposed upon us by our humanity. It may seem that those who have held one of the most powerful positions on earth were specially gifted with mental strength and stamina, unhindered by the challenges average citizens face. Yet nothing could be further from the truth.

Research conducted by Duke University Medical Center and published in the January 2006 edition of *The Journal of Nervous and Mental Disease* reports that many former United States presidents suffered from various mental illnesses. The researchers examined biographical data on the thirty-seven presidents who held office from 1776 through 1974 and found that just under half (49 percent) suffered form some form of psychological distress. By far the most common psychiatric disorder was depression (24 percent), followed by anxiety, bipolar disorder, and alcohol dependence (8 percent).[18]

In this study three researchers from Duke University's Department of Psychiatry examined historical records to identify symptoms of mental disorders. Once collected, these details

---

2001), 52.

17. Ibid.

18. Jonathan R. Davidson, Kathryn M. Connor, and Marvin Swartz, "Mental Illness in U.S. Presidents between 1776 and 1974; A Review of Biographical Sources," *The Journal of Nervous and Mental Disease,* 194, no. 1 (January 2006): 47–51.

were examined by independent psychiatrists, who viewed the presidents' reported behaviors in light of the Diagnostic and Statistical Manual of Mental Disorders (DSM-IV) criteria for psychiatric disorders. The DSM has become the "bible" of mental health disorders and is used by professionals to diagnose psychological illnesses. It is important to keep in mind that "diagnosing" a person through historical records leaves great room for criticism regarding the validity of the findings. However, what can be taken from such studies is the reality that no one is above life's physical and mental challenges. At the same time those who have gained earthly power have affirmed the critical importance of character in life.

Perhaps the most striking example of character impacting mental perseverance is found in the life of Abraham Lincoln. He is considered by both scholars and the general public to be one of the greatest presidents, living a remarkable life in spite of psychological challenges. It is now historically established that Lincoln suffered from major depression most of his adult life. Lincoln's own words speak to the intense mental distress he experienced.

> I am now the most miserable man living. If what I feel were equally distributed to the whole human family there would not be one cheerful face on earth. Whether I shall ever be better, I cannot tell. I awfully forebode I shall not. To remain as I am is impossible. I must die or be better it appears to me.[19]

Yet no other President has had so much literature devoted to his life, and Lincoln's speeches continue to be recognized as among the greatest orations in American history. There is no secret to his continued influence: Lincoln exemplified *character*. He em-

---

19. John G. Nicolay and John Hay, eds., *Abraham Lincoln; Complete Works Comprising His Speeches, Letters, State Papers, and Miscellaneous Writings* (New York: The Century Co., 1902), 45.

braced high ideals and—despite a life marked by challenge and difficulty—lived those beliefs.

Lincoln was born into what today would be considered poverty and raised by a caring though uneducated father. Lincoln lost his mother when he was only nine, and he received about one year of formal education. After working a variety of jobs, he studied and practiced law, gaining a reputation as one of the most accomplished lawyers in Illinois. His marriage to Mary Todd Lincoln was trying because she suffered from frail psychological health as well. His early political career was marked by a series of electorate defeats, yet this man was able to overcome intense political turmoil with the stakes being nothing less than winning the Civil War. The "Great Emancipator" not only faced and put an end to the tragic practice of slavery in our country, but he also faced heartbreaking personal loss in the death of his twelve-year-old son, Willie.

In spite of such incredible challenges Abraham Lincoln developed and maintained a depth of character that resonates throughout our society even today. His wit and light-heartedness endeared him to constituents, and he spoke with a humble, self-depreciating integrity. His character was formed in large part from his religious beliefs. Although never endorsing any particular Christian doctrine, he was an avid reader of the Bible. His speeches are replete with invocations for God's protection. In 1863 he proclaimed a day of national humiliation, prayer, and fasting.

> We have forgotten the gracious hand which has preserved us in peace and multiplied and enriched and strengthened us; and have vainly imagined, in the deceitfulness of our hearts, that all these blessings were produced by some superior wisdom and virtue of our own. Intoxicated with unbroken success, we have become too self-sufficient to feel the necessity

> of redeeming and preserving grace, too proud to
> pray to the God that made us.[20]

While examples of his wisdom and courage were many, his graciousness was clearly revealed during his second inaugural address. The North had won the War, the South was defeated and in disarray. Many Yankees were looking to this speech as not only an affirmation of victory, but also expecting to hear condemnation of the Rebels for their sins. Lincoln's character showed as he began to heal the wounds of a broken nation.

> With malice toward none, with charity for all, with firmness in the right as God gives us to see the right, let us strive on to finish the work we are in, to bind up the nation's wounds, to care for him who shall have borne the battle and for his widow and his orphan, to do all which may achieve and cherish a just, and lasting peace, among ourselves, and with all nations.[21]

The life of "Honest Abe," while extraordinary, tells of the power of character and values that is available to every individual.

---

20. Abraham Lincoln, "Proclamation Appointing a National Fast Day," Washington, D.C., March 30, 1863. John T. Woolley and Gerhard Peters, The American Presidency Project, [online], Santa Barbara, CA, University of California (hosted), Gerhard Peters (database). Available online, document archive, "Abraham Lincoln," 1999-2008, http://www.presidency.ucsb.edu/ws/index.php?pid=69891&st=&st1=.

21. Abraham Lincoln, Second Inaugural address, March 4, 1865. John T. Woolley and Gerhard Peters, The American Presidency Project, [online], Santa Barbara, CA, University of California (hosted), Gerhard Peters (database). Available online, document archive, "Abraham Lincoln," 1999-2008, http://www.presidency.ucsb.edu/ws/index.php?pid=69891&st=&st1=.

> *"Too many leaders act as if the sheep . . . their people . . .*
> *are there for the benefit of the shepherd,*
> *not that the shepherd has responsibility for the sheep."*[22]
>
> —KEN BLANCHARD

> *"In the last analysis, what we are communicates far more eloquently*
> *than anything we say or do. We all know it.*
> *There are people we trust absolutely*
> *because we know their character."*[23]
>
> —STEPHEN R. COVEY

Business

Politics is not the only arena that requires moral courage; the importance of integrity can be found in good business management and leadership practices. Dated business management practices used well into the twentieth century relied upon rank, power, and status: management dictated; subordinates obeyed. Even early scholarly attempts to understand effective management were one-dimensional and limited to identifying those traits or characteristics that make someone a good manager or leader.

Fortunately, this kind of linear thinking has evolved during the past several decades. One of those responsible for advancing effective leadership thinking in business is Warren Bennis, the founding chairman of The Leadership Institute at the University of Southern California. Bennis breaks with many of the rigid historical ideas of leadership. Acknowledging his position as a

22. American Management Association, "Learn How to Bring Out the Best in Your Team Members by Bringing Out the Best in Your Leadership Ability," exclusive AMA interview, copyright 1997–2008, http://www.amanet.org/editorial/blanchard.htm.

23. Stephen R. Covey, *The 7 Habits of Highly Effective People: Powerful Lessons in Personal Change* (New York: Fireside Book, 1989), 22. Emphasis in original.

leading theorist exploring the principles of effective management (*Forbes* magazine crowned him "Dean of Leadership Gurus"), he argues that much of the academic work regarding leadership has been of little value. In the 1980s Bennis spent close to five years researching a book on leadership by traveling the country and interviewing successful leaders in both the public and private sectors, and he distilled his findings to one overriding principle that differentiates leaders from managers: "The manager does things right; the leader does the right thing."[24] He found that many who obtain positions of top management in both public and private sectors acquire their status through a lust for power, as opposed to a desire to serve.

The core of the problem, according to Bennis, is the narcissistic attitude that has saturated our culture, developing parallel to technological advances such as cell phones, computers, automobiles, televisions, and gaming systems. This cultural evolution dilutes much of the traditional sense of community and public virtue, since many now seek only self gratification. Bennis not only describes this devolution, but he also points to psychology's cultural influence on our society. He writes, "While the 1960s saw the birth of such important contributions to our country as the civil rights movement and the women's movement, too many of its so-called breakthroughs became breakdowns. We talked about freedom and democracy, but we practiced license and anarchy. People weren't as interested in new ideas as they were in recipes and slogans. Gurus Abraham Maslow and Carl Rogers told us we could create our own reality, and we did, with everyone insisting on having it his way."[25] Bennis argues that there are not enough leaders with character who pay attention

---

24. Warren G. Bennis, *On Becoming a Leader* (New York: Addison Wesley, 1989), 5.

25. Ibid., 19.

to doing the right thing. The author lays part of this shortcoming on our higher educational system, which provides technical instruction about management but fails to prepare individuals for leadership.

Steven Covey has also been influential in highlighting the importance of integrity and effective business practices. He argues that there are natural principles that guide organizational relationships just are there are governing principles in the physical world—such as the laws of gravity and motion or a compass needle pointing toward true north. When these principles are violated, people and companies experience negative consequences, but when these tenets are followed the outcome is typically positive. He describes this phenomenon as "principle-centered leadership,"[26] which can be conceptualized as a concentric circle with four spheres moving from the center toward the exterior. These levels or rankings include the personal, interpersonal, managerial, and organizational. The personal level—who I understand myself to be—is at the center and anchors all the rest. Covey argues that the key principle here is trustworthiness, which "is based on *character*, what you are as a person, and *competence*, what you can do (emphasis in original)." He suggests that both personal integrity and job proficiency are the foundation for effective management, and that "Trust—or the lack of it—is at the root of success or failure in relationships and in the bottom-line results of business, industry, education, and government."[27]

After an in-depth study of success literature since the founding of our nation, Covey has also concluded that shortly after World War I our society experienced a cultural shift from life based on character to an existence focused on image, deft

---

26. Stephen Covey, *Principle-Centered Leadership* (New York: Fireside Book, 1990), 18.

27. Ibid., 31.

social skills, and self-interest. He calls this later approach to success the Personality Ethic. In comparing the difference between life principles based on genuine character and the veneer that often doubles as personality, Covey writes, "In stark contrast, almost all of the literature in the first one hundred fifty years or so focused on what could be called the *Character Ethic* as the foundation of successes—things like integrity, humility, fidelity, temperance, courage, justice, patience, industry, simplicity, modesty, and the Golden Rule" (emphasis in original).[28]

These ideas regarding character in business have lead to two dominant paradigms of business management: the servant-leader and the transformational leadership models. The paradoxical term servant-leadership was developed by Robert Greenleaf and grew from his belief that authentic leaders are first servants to others, a role that is the key to the leader's ability to influence others. The servant leader makes the choice to serve others first, placing that goal before the desire to lead. These types of managers seek to help their subordinates grow to a higher personal and professional level and potentially become servant leaders themselves. This leadership model deliberately places *service* as the primary objective, as opposed to pursuing power and control, which marks more traditional styles of management. Service is emphasized with customers, employees, and extends to the community in which a person lives.

The transformational leadership model was introduced by James Burns[29] and Bernard Bass, who are considered to be key thinkers who have advanced the principles of effective organizational change.[30] It also distances itself from the rigid

28 Stephen R. Covey, *The 7 Habits of Highly Effective People: Powerful Lessons in Personal Change* (New York: Fireside Book, 1989), 18.

29. James M. Burns, *Leadership*. (New York: Harper & Row, 1978).

30. Bernard M. Bass, *Leadership and Performance Beyond Expectation* (New York: Free Press, 1985).

styles of administration that separate employees from their supervisors. The transformational leader seeks to respect and empower subordinates as a means to inspire the best customer care. Transformational leadership differs from the more traditional style of management known as transactional leadership. Transactional forms of management are marked by the leader and follower having ongoing exchanges based on reciprocity, expectancy, and goal accomplishment. Leaders reward followers for meeting agreed upon expectations or identify mistakes and administer corrective measures when necessary. Transformational leadership, in contrast, seeks to inspire meaning and develop a vision for the future that transcends the status quo. This approach to leadership speaks to the importance of character, as highlighted in an article titled "Ethics, Character, and Authentic Transformational Leadership" co-authored by Bass. The authors write, "In leadership, character matters. This is not to deny that evil people can bring about good things, or that good people can lead the way to moral ruin. Rather, leadership provides a moral compass and, over the long term, both personal development and the common good are best served by a moral compass that reads true."[31] The transformational approach to management is considered the epitome of current leadership thinking.

It would be difficult to cite an example of a successful business that does *not* recognize the importance of values and character for employees and leaders. This should come as no surprise, especially when considering infamous corporate scandals such as Tyco, World-Com, and Enron. A quick visit to corporate

31. Bernard M. Bass and Paul Steidlmeier, "Ethics, Character, and Authentic Transformational Leadership," Center for Leadership Studies, School of Management, Binghamton University, Binghamton, NY, September 24, 1998, https://www.vanguard.edu/uploadedFiles/Faculty/RHeuser/ETHICS,%20MORAL%20CHARACTER%20AND%20AUTHENTIC%20TRANSFORMATIONAL%20LEADERSHIP.pdf.

Web sites reveals the standard of integrity that is now common among virtually all top companies. Sam Palmisano, IBM's chairman, president, and chief executive officer, begins his open letter to employees and customers by speaking about a moral code and leadership. He writes,

> Today, many businesses are newly discovering the importance of ethics, corporate responsibility and the multiple ways in which they are part of a wider ecosystem . . . For us at IBM, this is much more than a matter of legal compliance or even "giving back to the community." It is and has always been integral to how we conceive of ourselves as a business.[32]

> *"Business! Mankind was my business. The common welfare was my business;*
> *charity, mercy, forbearance, and benevolence, were, all, my business.*
> *The dealings of my trade were but a drop of water in the comprehensive ocean of my business!"*
>
> —Ghost of Jacob Marley
> In *A Christmas Carol*

---

32. Samuel J. Palmisano, "IBM Corporate Social Responsibility: Innovation that Matters to the World," IBM Corporate Citizenship and Corporate Affairs, United States, copyright IBM 2007, online at http ://www.ibm.com/ibm/ibmgives/downloads/CCCAOverview2007.pdf.

Sports

*"An Aggie does not lie, cheat,
or steal or tolerate those who do."*[33]

—AGGIE HONOR CODE,
TEXAS A & M UNIVERSITY

Business and sports share many similarities. Perhaps the two most obvious are that both thrive on competition, and both rely upon honesty as foundational to their existence. They differ in that the business arena is more complex, with competition taking place in a free-market society. Athletic competition, on the other hand, takes place on a condensed and literal field of battle. Like business, which must at least appear evenhanded to survive, sporting events rely on the integrity of players as their cornerstone. Isn't it ironic that in a society that has become more permissive we continue to enjoy sports, which rely on non-negotiable rules? Can you imagine watching a baseball game where each batter could decide how many strikes he was allowed to have before being called out? How about a basketball playoff game where the referees decided how many points to award to each basket? Either the principles of integrity, honesty, and fairness are laid down as foundational or such events become absurd.

An additional attraction to sports for many people is its close relationship to character. Most coaches—from soccer, to gymnastics, or tennis—prepare their athletes for competition by invoking some credo of courage, sacrifice, spirit, or old-fashioned "guts." Is there a high school football coach who has *not* sent his team off to battle with some words of wisdom summoning confidence? The history of sports is rich with stories of great performances and acts of heroism that inspire others.

33. Texas A & M University, "Aggie Honor Code," student rules, http://student-rules.tamu.edu/aggiecode.html.

In 1936 a black American athlete named Jesse Owens single-handedly shattered Hitler's mirage of Arian supremacy by amassing four track and field gold medals and establishing three world records and one Olympic record. Three years later one of the greatest baseball players of all time faced a crowd of 60,000 and described himself as "the luckiest man in the world," knowing full well he was dying from a terminal illness that has since been named "Lou Gehrig Disease." A woman named Marla Runyan finished third in the qualifying time trials of the 1500 meter race for the 2000 United States Olympic team. Marla Runyan was legally blind. Examples of personal courage are literally everywhere in sports and are part of what makes athletic competition so attractive for both competitor and fan.

Sports parallel life. Struggle, success, failure, and victory mark both experiences. It is precisely these contrasting experiences that fashion who we become. Weight lifting breaks down and destroys muscle fibers within the body. Yet when at rest these same weakened fibers respond by growing in size and strength, making an athlete more powerful than before.

The same is true of character. Those who have sacrificed and committed themselves to high standards of performance can most appreciate the value of excellence. That is not to suggest that athletics does not lend itself to prima donna mentality, or those who confuse gifted ability with self-ascribed importance. That is a predictable happening in a materialistic society such as ours. While professional sports may show the selfish side of success, they also display what's best—as can be seen in the person of basketball great David Robinson.

Robinson, nicknamed "Admiral," is one of the best centers to have ever played the game of basketball. His accomplishments and awards seem endless. A fractional list includes 1987 graduate of the United States Naval Academy; 1990 NBA Rookie of the Year; 1992 Defensive Player of the Year; 1995 League MVP;

1996 named as one of the "50 Greatest Players of all Time"; 1988, 1992, and 1996 Olympian; 1999 won first NBA championship with the San Antonio Spurs; 2003 won second NBA championship with the Spurs; and 10-time NBA "All Star."

As impressive as Robinson's career was, there are hundreds of other female and male athletes who have etched their place as a sports legend. What separates "Admiral" from most others has been what he's done with his success. He gave back to others in a big way. In 1991 Robinson visited the Gates Elementary School in San Antonio and challenged a fifth-grade class to complete their high school education and study at college, offering a two thousand dollar scholarship for all who did. Seven years later Robinson broke his word, giving eight thousand dollars to each student who met the challenge. This was just the beginning. In 2001 he and his wife founded the Carver Academy, a private, non-profit pre-kindergarten to sixth-grade school assisting economically and socially disadvantaged youth.

The Carver Academy is named after George Washington Carver, the famed early twentieth century educator and agricultural researcher. Dr. Carver (1864–1943) was chosen as a role model for the school not so much for his intellectual brilliance as who he was. He was born a slave and did not learn to read and write until about the age of twenty. Yet he was able to work his way through high school and college, obtaining a Master of Science degree in 1896. He was a faculty member and directed the Department of Agricultural Research at the Tuskegee Institute of Alabama. His amazing work as a botanist led to his discovery of 325 products that were derived from the peanut and helped to establish a major American industry.

Carver's professional success, while remarkable in itself considering he lived during the time of segregation in the United States, is eclipsed by his integrity. He would not accept a one hundred dollar gift from a manufacturer who had used one of his discoveries, viewing his work as service to humanity. He was offered numerous job opportunities that would have increased both his income and reputation, but he declined in favor of serving the greater good. Near the end of his life Dr. Carver donated his life savings to fund a research program in creative chemistry. He believed that a person's character is what matters most in life and serves as the foundation for individual success. Dr. Carver taught his students eight guiding principles.[34]

1. Be clean both inside and out.
2. Who neither looks up to the rich or down on the poor.
3. Who loses, if need be, without squealing.
4. Who wins without bragging.
5. Who is always considerate of women, children and old people.
6. Who is too brave to lie.
7. Who is too generous to cheat.
8. Who takes his share of the world and lets other people have theirs.

Taking inspiration from his life and adhering to these same principles, the Carver Academy provides its youngsters with an education that goes beyond schoolwork, developing the whole person. The Academy's mission statement declares that its graduates "will be prepared for success in the nation's most competitive high schools and will display the highest levels of leadership, discipline, initiative, and integrity." To accomplish this goal the Carver Academy provides academic instruction and

---

34. Brenda Murphy, Head of School, The Carver Academy, San Antonio, TX, online brochure at http://www.thecarveracademy.com/public/carver.nsf/generalcontent/SWBV-62WQ6B?opendocument.

ensures each child's "social, emotional, and spiritual needs are also addressed to develop all aspects of the child."[35]

Each student's character is developed by instilling six core qualities—leadership, discipline, initiative, integrity, service, and faith.[36] These pillars form what is known as the "Carver Code" and are taught as part of a six-week educational program. It is through these ideals that the Academy encourages students, many of whom are considered "at-risk," to become young women and men of character and to live as good citizens. Ninety-eight percent of the students receive a scholarship to fund their education. The students have scored well on standardized tests, and the Academy has received international recognition as an educational model to emulate.

A NEW MODEL—POSITIVE PSYCHOLOGY

These examples from politics, business, and sports serve as simple testaments to the universality of character—moral excellence. Endless evidence illustrates the foundational importance of virtuous living, whether or not it is recognized in our affluent society where materialism reigns supreme and relativism dictates the social conscious.

Thankfully character, like faith, is again finding its place in mental wellness. There are two underlying reasons for its growing acceptance. First, psychology recognizes that traditional mental health treatments tend to be minimally effective. Second, there is no longer any doubt that character is integral to success and

---

35. Brenda Murphy, Head of School, The Carver Academy, San Antonio, TX, online brochure at http://www.thecarveracademy.com/public/carver.nsf/generalcontent/SWBV-62WPZY?opendocument.

36. Brenda Murphy, Head of School, The Carver Academy, San Antonio, TX, online brochure at http://www.thecarveracademy.com/public/carver.nsf/generalcontent/SWBV-62WPGX?opendocument

fulfillment in nearly every worthwhile pursuit, including good mental hygiene. To dismiss its relevance for those who suffer from psychological distress will render many well-meaning interventions feeble at best.

One of the more recent branches within mental health studies is known as "positive psychology." This new model has taken root as an increasingly popular alternative to the traditional understanding of behavioral health. Still in its infancy, positive psychology is "a new branch of psychology which focuses on the empirical study of such things as positive emotions, strengths-based character, and healthy institutions."[37] Martin Seligman, the father of positive psychology, based much of his theory on research he describes as "learned helplessness." Learned helplessness is defined as a form of apathy resulting from the conditioned belief that others will resolve your problems for you. This kind of thinking has been held as a model to explain the growing prevalence of depression in the United States.

Seligman, a past president of the American Psychological Association, has been clear about the dominantly negative, pathological lens through which psychologists have historically viewed patients and the vital need to refocus and identify what makes people mentally healthy. In a 1998 address to the APA titled "Building Human Strength: Psychology's Forgotten Mission," Seligman describes how psychology changed after World War II. He recounts a shift in focus from treating mental illness *and* promoting a fulfilling, joyful life toward learning *exclusively* to human flaws. A primary reason for this shift was the creation of the Veterans Administration in 1946 and the National Institute of Mental Health in 1947, which enabled field psychologists to

---

37. "Dr. Martin Seligman is director of the University of Pennsylvania Positive Psychology Center," Authentic Happiness, copyright 2006 the trustees of the University of Pennsylvania, http://www.authentichappiness.sas.upenn.edu.

earn a living treating mental illness while research psychologists obtained grants to explore psychological disorders. Little attention was given to what makes people well. While there has been meaningful progress in treating psychological distress, such an extreme spotlight on human frailty has led to a pathetic worldview. Seligman addresses these shortcomings in psychology.

> We became victimology. Human beings were seen as passive foci: Stimuli came on and elicited "responses," or external "reinforcements" weakened or strengthened the "responses," or conflicts from childhood pushed the human being around. Viewing the human being as essentially passive, psychologists treated mental illness within a theoretical framework of repairing damaged habits, damaged drives, damaged childhoods and damaged brains. Fifty years later, I want to remind our field that it has been sidetracked. Psychology is not just the study of weakness and damage, it is also the study of strength and virtue. Treatment is not just fixing what is broken, it is nurturing what is best within ourselves . . . We have discovered that there is a set of human strengths that are the most likely buffers against mental illness: courage, optimism, interpersonal skill, work ethic, hope, honesty and perseverance.[38]

This is an extremely refreshing perspective, bringing balance and encouragement back into what has become a parched view of human nature. Positive psychology does not minimize the ache of psychological distress or dismiss the healing and nurturing power of virtue.

---

38. Martin E. Seligman, "Building Human Strength: Psychology's Forgotten Mission," *American Psychological Association Monitor* 29, no. 1 (January 1988): 2.

This approach to behavioral health has begun to take hold. Most of psychiatry and psychology is guided by the Diagnostic and Statistical Manual (DSM) of Mental Disorders. This massive document, now in its fourth edition, details an ever-growing list of mental symptoms and illnesses. The first DSM, published in 1952, was 130 pages and contained 106 mental health diagnoses. The DSM IV was published in 1994 and had grown to 886 pages, detailing 297 diagnoses. In 2004 Seligman, along with Christopher Peterson, published a "manual of the sanities," examining in great detail character traits and qualities that are fundamental to mental wellness. This pivotal work, titled *Character Strengths and Virtues: A Handbook and Classification*, was jointly published by Oxford Press and the American Psychological Association.[39] This is one of the first modern efforts to scientifically identify universal character traits that enable people to lead rich, fulfilling lives. The traits are distilled into six core virtues: wisdom, courage, humanity, justice, temperance, and transcendence. These virtues are further broken down into twenty-four character strengths that enable people to live well.

These characteristics were identified largely from the values championed by the great cultures and religions in the world. The authors specifically note that their list aligns with the Seven Heavenly Virtues (wisdom, courage, justice, temperance, faith, hope, and charity) put forth by Saint Thomas Aquinas. Saint Thomas Aquinas was a Catholic philosopher and theologian, and he was considered one of the great doctors of the Catholic Church.

Character traits are often the very condition sought after. Virtues are the "other side of the coin" of many emotional problems. Those suffering depression search for joy. Anxious

---

39. Christopher Peterson and Martin E. Seligman, *Character Strengths and Virtues: A Handbook and Classification* (New York: Oxford University Press, 2004).

people would rather experience life bravely. Those who battle with lethargy pine for vitality. The irritable seek the relief of humor. Disinterested people crave purpose. That is not to make the case that mental stress is always a matter of simple attitude. Addressing mental health issues is complex because each individual is unique and influenced by diverse factors. A person's upbringing, temperament, biological makeup, life experiences, belief system, and relationships are a few of the factors that influence how people experience life.

It is revitalizing to see that virtue is again being given a seat at the psychological table of wellness. Psychological journals are no longer fearful to engage in meaningful research exploring how such values enhance mental health. In 2006 the Journal of Cognitive Psychotherapy published a series of articles examining this topic. One of these articles, "On the Integration of Cognitive-Behavioral Therapy for Depression and Positive Psychology" describes the relevance of hope, mindfulness, optimism, humor, purpose in life, and physical exercise as behavioral principles that counter depression.[40]

Writers and researchers are making applications of their findings available to those interested. One leading resource is the Values in Action (VIA) Institute on Character (www.viastrengths.org), a nonprofit organization dedicated to studying and sharing information regarding values, character, and wellness. Among the many resources offered by this organization is the VIA survey which identifies and describes key individual character strengths that help people live abundant, happy lives.

---

40. Leslie Karwoski, Genevieve M. Garratt, and Stephen S. Ilardi, "On the Integration of Cognitive-Behavioral Therapy for Depression and Positive Psychology," *Journal of Cognitive Psychotherapy: An International Quarterly* 20, no. 2 (2006): 159–69.

> *"Joy is not covered by insurance,
> nor does it lead to tenure."*[41]
>
> —Martin Seligman

ONCE OLD, NOW NEW

> *"Be not afraid of life. Believe that life is worth living,
> and your belief will help create the fact."*[42]
>
> —William James

Principles such as those taught by the Carver Academy are powerful because they are timeless. They are now seen as basic elements within many models for youth development in an educational setting, and they have been embraced by mothers, fathers, teachers, coaches, girl scout and boy scout leaders, soldiers, statesmen, and just about anyone who sensibly hopes to guide and nurture others. Yet while character is universally recognized as essential to living a good life, psychology has mostly dismissed its relevance because such principles share common territory with virtues championed by traditional religions. This takes us back to the idea that psychology has undergone great pain to be respected like the medical sciences. The resulting attitude can be seen in the following simple analogy.

---

41. Trish Hall, *The New York Times,* "Seeking a Focus on Joy In Field of Psychology," April 28, 1998, http://query.nytimes.com/gst/fullpage.html?res=9C03E4D91E3FF93BA15757C0A96E958260.

42. William James, *The Will to Believe and Other Essays in Popular Philosophy,* "Is Life Worth Living?" (Girard, KS: Haldeman-Julius Publications, 1948), 62. Available online at Questia Media America, Inc., http://www.questia.com/PM.qst?a=o&d=101949511. This citation from Laurence G. Boldt, *Zen Soup: Tasty Morsels of Wisdom from Great Minds East & West* (New York: Penguin Arkana, 1997), 19.

The year I turned forty several friends and I played basketball each morning. On one particular play I rebounded the ball and pushed off with my right foot to make a layup, but fell to the ground with the sensation that someone had stepped on the back of my sneaker. As I looked up I thought it odd that no one was within several yards of me and my friends had a wry, pitiful look on their faces. They said they had heard the "pop" of my Achilles tendon as it tore from my bone. Fortunately, one of my best friends happens to be an orthopedic surgeon. He expertly operated on me the next day to repair the injury. With physical therapy the ligament would mend in a specific, scientific manner—uninfluenced by deceit, honesty, vengeance, mercy, selfishness, gratitude, indifference, or love. Psychology has tried to force these same principles upon mental health, suggesting that mental distress must also arise from diagnostically identifiable causes, and should be cured through prescriptive rationality or medication—apart from morals and character traits.

Psychology seems to have come full circle in the one hundred fifty years since it left the shadows of philosophy to establish itself as an independent science. For much of that time religious and spiritual beliefs were deemed by the sophisticated elite to be contemptible ramblings of the unschooled. However, divorcing itself from irreplaceable human principles left a void that treatment models and medications were unable to fill.

The scientific rediscovery of faith and character as contributors to wellness will hopefully eliminate the perception that the "secrets" of good mental health are beyond the realm of the average person. What's more, after decades of weakness-focused treatment, we have learned that human beings are simply uninspired by technique and stale reason. We have been given a mysterious gift that is finite, lasting the better part of a century for those so fortunate. While we all share its common biological ending, how we experience our journey greatly depends on what we as individuals believe our reason for being here is all about.

> *No heaven can come to us*
> *unless our hearts find rest in it today.*
> *Take heaven!*
>
> *No peace lies in the future which is not*
> *hidden in this present little instant.*
> *Take peace!*
>
> *The gloom of the world is but a shadow.*
> *Behind it, yet within our reach, is joy.*
> *There is radiance and glory in darkness, but we could see.*
> *And to see, we only have to look.*
> *I beseech you to look!*
>
> *Courage then to claim it; that is all!*[43]
>
> —Fra Giovanni Giocondo
> fifteenth-century Monk
> In a letter to Countess Allagia Aldobrandeschi

---

43. Fra Giovanni Giocondo, letter to Countess Allagia Aldobrandeschi, Italy, December 24, 1513. Complete letter available online at Gratefulness.org, a Network for Grateful Living, http://www.gratefulness.org/readings/fra_giovanni.htm.

www.ingramcontent.com/pod-product-compliance
Lightning Source LLC
Chambersburg PA
CBHW071443160426
43195CB00013B/2014